PROGRESSIVE
Skills

Reading

Course Book & Workbook

Terry Phillips and Anna Phillips

Published by
Garnet Publishing Ltd.
8 Southern Court
South Street
Reading RG1 4QS, UK

First edition 2012

ISBN: 978-1-90861-414-8

British Library Cataloguing-in-Publication Data
A catalogue record for this book is available from
the British Library.

Production

Project managers:	Richard Peacock, Nicky Platt
Editorial team:	Emily Clarke, Richard Peacock, Nicky Platt, Rod Webb
Research:	Lucy Phillips
Design:	Christin Helen Auth, Neil Collier, Ed Du Bois, Mike Hinks
Illustration:	Neil Collier, Doug Nash
Photography:	Clipart, Corbis, Neil Collier, Istockphoto

Every effort has been made to trace the copyright holders
and we apologize in advance for any unintentional
omissions. We will be happy to insert the appropriate
acknowledgements in any subsequent editions.

Printed and bound
in Lebanon by International Press: interpress@int-press.com

PROGRESSIVE Skills

Contents

Course Book

Workbook

Book maps

Knowledge area	Skills	Grammar
1 Remembering and forgetting	*article with graph* • recognizing sentence function • reading line graphs	• the complex noun phrase
2 Friends and family	*article with diagram* • distinguishing between fact and theory	• leading prepositional phrases
3 Managing to be successful	*article with table* • understanding non-text markers	• identifying missing subjects and verbs after co-ordinator
4 Natural cycles	*encyclopedia entries* • using cross referencing	• finding key information after *which / that*
5 Customs: origins and effects	*newspaper article* • recognizing the writer's point of view or bias	• conditionals: zero and first (revision)

Topic	Texts
1 Improving your memory	• Can you remember things forever? • How can you remember things for a test?
2 Parents, Adults and Children	• Are you a Parent, an Adult or a Child? • I'm OK, you're OK
3 Decisions, decisions, decisions	• 'Digest' problems to make good decisions • Are you an autocrat or a democrat?
4 Chains, webs and pyramids	• extracts from a science encyclopedia
5 The price of happiness	• Can couples afford to get married anymore? • The girl who said NO!

Introduction

This is Level 3 of *Progressive Skills: Reading*. This course is in four levels, from Intermediate to Advanced. In addition, there is a remedial / false beginner course, *Starting Skills*, for students who are not ready to begin Level 1.

Progressive Skills: Reading is designed to help students who are at university or about to enter a university where some or all of their course is taught in English. The course helps students in the skills of reading for research.

Progressive Skills: Reading is arranged in five themes, with five core lessons as follows:

Lesson 1: *Vocabulary for reading*
pre-teaches key vocabulary for the section

Lesson 2: *Real-time reading*
practises previously learnt skills and exposes students to new skills; in most cases, this lesson provides a model for the activity in Lesson 5

Lesson 3: *Learning new reading skills*
presents and practises new skills

Lesson 4: *Grammar for reading*
presents and practises key grammar points for the skill

Lesson 5: *Applying new reading skills*
provides practice in the skills and grammar from the section; in most cases, students work on a parallel task to the one presented in Lesson 2

Theme 1

Remembering and forgetting

- Improving your memory

Remembering and forgetting

1.1 Vocabulary for reading   Internal and external factors

A   Reviewing words

Complete the text with the correct word beginning with *re* in each case.

The other day I noticed a new *re* search assistant in the laboratory. We were at school together. I *re_____* his face but I couldn't *re_____* his name. I suddenly *re_____* it a few days later. I was *re_____* some notes about memory on my computer. I saw the name *Miller*. That *re_____* me of my friend's name – Adam Miller. So that's a real-life example of how we *re_____* information from the brain.

B   Understanding new words in context

Read the summary of a survey. Look at the answers to the question with the number of people giving each answer. Complete the summary with the correct noun in each space.

I investigated the internal and external factors which affect *concentration*. There were ten participants from the university. All of them said that the main problem was _____. Other internal factors were also important. Four of them talked about _____, and three mentioned _____ and _____. Two people referred to external factors. One complained about _____ and one mentioned _____ in her study area.

Q: What prevents you from concentrating?
A: I get bored. (10)
A: I get tired. (4)
A: I get thirsty. (3)
A: I get hungry. (3)
A: My chair is uncomfortable. (1)
A: My study area is noisy. (1)

C   Understanding new phrases in context

Read the beginning of each sentence. How could each sentence continue?

1. He doesn't have a very good attention span so …
2. Concentration falls steeply when …
3. You need to have a complete picture of the situation before you …
4. Sometimes it is difficult to concentrate on …

---

a complete picture
a great deal of
attention span
bored *(adj)*
boredom *(n)*
concentrate on *(v)*
decrease *(v)*
discomfort *(n)*
efficient *(adj)*
fixed *(adj)* [= attached]
forever *(adv)*
gradually *(adv)*
hunger *(n)*
increase *(v)*
initial *(adj)*
internal / external
    factor
interval *(n)*
loss *(n)*
natural process
note *(v)*
overall *(adv)*
physical factor
remain *(v)*
steeply *(adv)*
the exact reason
the human brain
thirst *(n)*
tiredness *(n)*
vary *(v)*

A   Activating ideas

Discuss these questions.

1. What was the last academic test you did?
2. Did you get the grade you wanted? Why (not)?

B   Predicting content

1. Look at the title of the text opposite. What is your answer to the question?
2. Mark these statements true (T) or false (F).
   a. ☐F☐ Modern scientists understand how human memory works.
   b. ☐ Reviewing information helps you remember it.
   c. ☐ We review information about our lives without thinking.
   d. ☐ A student needs to review the same information every day.
   e. ☐ Without review, you will forget about 90 per cent of the information in a month.
   f. ☐ It is not possible to remember 100 per cent of information for six months.
   g. ☐ You should pay attention to connections between ideas when you study.

C   Understanding the paragraph structure

Read the text opposite and look at Figure 1. Complete the gaps in the text with these sentences.

1. The need to repeat this process many times was first described in the 1930s by Cecil Mace.

2. After a month, only about ten per cent remains.

3. Note that the same line is at a level of only 20 per cent after six months.

4. However, science has not discovered the exact reason for this.

5. Take, for example, how to ride a bicycle, a very happy event in your life, or the way to your home.

6. So make connections with other pieces of knowledge when you review information.

7. You must continue to retrieve information if you want to remember it forever.

8. We call this *revision*.

D   Understanding the text

Explain **why** each statement in Exercise B is true or false, using information from the text.

E   Working with vocabulary

1. What part of speech is each highlighted word?
2. Suggest a definition for each one.
3. Think of a word to replace each one.

Can you remember things forever?

Do you remember everything that you learnt at school? Everybody knows that the human brain cannot remember everything. However, science has not discovered the exact reason for this. We do not have a complete picture of human memory.

Forgetting is a natural process. In Figure 1, the red line on the graph shows that, within 24 hours of learning, you have forgotten nearly 80 per cent of the new information. _____ _____ In Education, we need to consider how to mitigate this loss of information.

Research shows that revision is the key. You must take the information out of your memory, use it, and store it again, several times. Then it will become fixed, and it will stay in your memory for years. _____

_____ Mace's theory was later used to design a novel system of flashcards for learning languages (Leitner, 2003).

In everyday life, we repeat this cycle of retrieval–use–storage without thinking. _____ _____

You have retrieved that information hundreds of times so you have not forgotten it. In the field of academic study, the repetition comes from recall. In other words, the student purposely finds the information in their memory, brings it out and reviews it. Then he/she stores it again. _____ _____

_____

Each retrieval should happen at a longer interval, according to the idea of 'spaced repetition' (Mace, 1932). The first review is very important and should be after only ten minutes. As the blue line on the graph shows, this review actually boosts memory to 100 per cent. However, if you do not look at the information again, you still forget nearly everything. _____ _____

Review the information again after, say, one day, one month and then six months (see the green line on the graph). You will then remember the information forever.

Since the 1960s, new research has indicated that information is connected in our memory. The connections have two important features. Firstly, we can retrieve groups of connected ideas more readily than single ideas.

_____

Secondly, if you retrieve and store information often, the connections become stronger. So it is better to spend a short time on retrieval every few weeks rather than a long time on retrieval every few months.

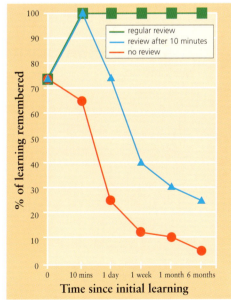

Figure 1: *% of learning remembered with and without 'spaced repetition'*
Source: Education Research Council

1.3 Learning new reading skills   Dealing with research texts

A Reviewing vocabulary

Complete the words in the table. All of the words are from the text in Lesson 1.2.

1.	several	6.	rep
2.	int	7.	lo
3.	ret	8.	fi
4.	rem	9.	st
5.	for	10.	rev

B Identifying a new skill (1)

1. Read Skills Check 1. What tense or verb form do we often use for general facts (GF), past facts (PF), predictions (P) and advice (A)?

2. Mark each sentence below GF, PF, P or A.
   a. ☐P The solution will become clear.
   b. ☐ You should do exercise once a week.
   c. ☐ The first king of a united England was Athelstan (899–1016 CE).
   d. ☐ This is a new area of research.
   e. ☐ Always carry a book in your bag.
   f. ☐ The company will expect you to meet customers.
   g. ☐ You must do all your tasks on time.
   h. ☐ You will probably lose contact with friends from early childhood.
   i. ☐ Average temperature falls as you move away from the Equator.
   j. ☐ The research was conducted by Atkinson and Shiffrin.

3. Mark the function of some sentences in the text in Lesson 1.2.

C Identifying a new skill (2)

1. Read Skills Check 2. How can a writer refer to graphs in the text?

2. Match the sentences below with the graphs on page 16.
   a. ☐ As the yellow line shows, the temperature rises quickly.
   b. ☐ Fig. 1 shows the initial results.
   c. ☐ … (see the red line in Figure 6).
   d. ☐ Note the change in speed at 30m.
   e. ☐ Note the pressure at 12 seconds (black line).
   f. ☐ The blue and orange lines in the graph are very similar.

Skills Check 1

Recognizing function

When you read a sentence, you must decide its **function**. The **verb tense** or **form** helps you to decide.

1. General facts – present simple
*Forgetting **is** a natural process.*

2. Past facts – past simple
*Mace's theory **was used** …*

3. Predictions – *will / may / might*
*You **will remember** the information forever.*

4. Advice – *must / imperative*
*You **must take** the information out of your memory. **Review** the information again after one month.*

Skills Check 2

Reading line graphs

Many academic texts include line graphs.

The writer usually **refers the reader to each graph**.

*This process continues (**see Fig. 3**).*
*The results **are shown in the graph below**.*

The writer often describes features of the graph.

***Note** the level after five seconds.*
***As** the blue line **shows**, …*

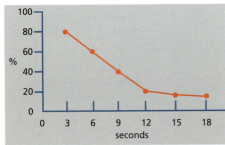

Fig. 1: % of three-letter combinations remembered

English uses a basic Subject-Verb-Object/Complement sentence structure.   ①

subject	verb	object / complement
Revision	is	the key.
We	repeat	this cycle.
You	won't forget	it.

In academic sentences, there is often extra information about the S and the O/C. The extra information can be before or after the main noun.

	extra info	subject	extra info	verb	object	extra info
The	red	line	on the graph	shows	the loss	of information.
		We		repeat	this cycle	of retrieve-use-store.

Find the S, the V and the O/C of a long sentence. Then find the extra information.

A   Identifying SVO structure

Mark the subject (S), verb (V) and object (O) in these sentences.

1. You have retrieved that information hundreds of times.
   <small>S   V   O</small>

2. You need a degree in Architecture.

3. Healthy people often eat low-fat snacks during the day.

4. China has an 18,000-kilometre-long coastline on the Yellow Sea and the China Sea.

5. The Internet is changing the relationship between businesses and customers.

6. The Black Death of 1348 killed thousands of people.

7. A successful magazine attracts a demographic group.

8. New students will probably have an introductory talk.

B   Identifying extra information

Circle the subject and object in the following sentences. Use arrows to show whether the extra information is about the subject or about the object.

1. American scientists at Cape Canaveral in the USA launched the first Space Shuttle.

2. The human body needs more than 40 different nutrients.

3. The Himalayas, a mountain range in Asia, contains the highest peaks on earth.

4. Archaeologists have discovered an early form of draughts.

5. Young men from ten of the teams take part in each race, which lasts only 90 seconds.

6. College and university Media Studies courses look at communication in the mass media.

7. Some modern teen magazines reflect the readers' self-image.

8. Websites for students do not always have complete or correct information.

A Reviewing vocabulary

Underline the correct form of the word in *italics* in each sentence.

1. We need to understand more about the *store / storage* of information in the brain.
2. You often remember very little if you are *tired / tiredness*. Your brain is not *efficiency / efficient* at those times.
3. You must *repetition / repeat* your review of information at regular intervals.
4. *Forgetting / forget* information is natural, but it can be avoided.
5. The key to effective learning is *revise / revision* at spaced intervals.
6. A lot of factors can *affect / effect* your concentration negatively.

B Activating ideas

You are going to read a text about revising for exams. What should you do:

- before you read the text?
- when you meet new vocabulary?
- after you have read it?

C Understanding a text

1. Read the text opposite. Do all the things you discussed in Exercise B.
2. Look at the highlighted sentences in the text. Circle the subject in each case.
3. In the following sentences from the text, circle the main noun and underline the extra information about the object.

A You probably do not notice any difference in your level of understanding during the revision period.

B There is a difference between understanding and memory.

C You should also vary the activity that you do during the breaks.

D As the green line shows, you will remember about 75 per cent of the information from the beginning of each session.

E There are also personal factors that define good revision.

F Note the level of the red line in Figure 2 after five hours.

D Understanding a graph

Look at Figure 2 and answer these questions.

1. Where does the graph come from?
2. What is shown by the red line and the green line?
3. What does the eighth green square tell us? And the sixth red triangle?
4. How is this graph similar to the one in Lesson 1.2?

E Critical thinking

1. After reading the two texts in this section, how can you change your own revision routine?
2. Both texts in this section give sources for their information. Why is this important?

How can you remember things for a test?

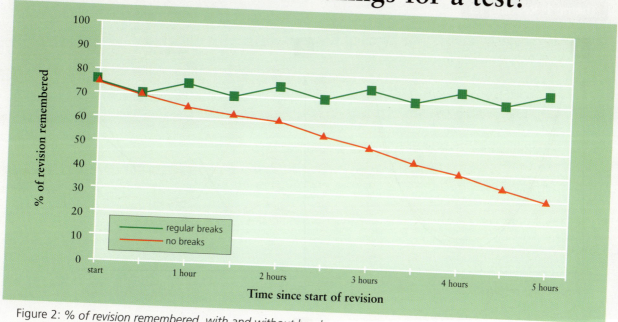

Figure 2: % of revision remembered, with and without breaks

Source: Education Research Council

Tests are extremely common in all forms of education. Most students work hard at revision to ensure that they do well in the test. But what is the best way to revise?

For successful revision, we need to understand brain processes during a period of study. One of the key questions is, in a test, which items do we remember better? Is it the things that we studied at the beginning of the revision period, or the things that we studied at the end?

Imagine you have to revise for a test. You decide to work from 9 a.m. until 2 p.m. You probably do not notice any difference in your level of understanding during the revision period. However, in the test, you will often remember better the things that you revised at 9.30 or 10.00 than the things you revised at 1.00 or 1.30.

The point is simple but very important. There is a difference between understanding and memory. Your level of *understanding* probably does not change much over the five hours. However, the percentage of information that you will *remember* falls steeply. Note the level of the red line in Figure 2 after five hours. During a very long session, internal factors start to affect your memory. A great deal of research has been done into these factors over the last 50 years (see Levinger & Clark 1961, Klein 1972, Laukenmann 2003). We all recognize the signs. You get bored, you start to feel hungry or uncomfortable, your mind feels tired, and your attention decreases.

The solution is simple. During a revision period, a student must take short, regular breaks. In the example of the five-hour revision period above, you should take a ten-minute break every hour. You should also vary the activity that you do during the breaks. Walk around, make a phone call, have a snack or go outside. Then you will have five short revision sessions instead of one long one. As the green line shows, you will remember about 75 per cent of the information from the beginning of each session. But over the five hours, that percentage stays the same. This is the important point. In each new session, the green line goes up again, because the tiredness, discomfort, hunger or boredom have gone. Recent research by Sengupta (2003) indicates that regular revision periods with breaks make a difference to test grades.

There are also personal factors that define good revision. The first factor is related to memory, which is more efficient at certain times of the day. The second is related to the student's learning style. Sometimes people remember more if they write notes. For other people, saying or hearing a recording of the information is more useful. Scientific opinion seems to be clear. Work regularly, take breaks and try to use revision exercises that suit your learning style. Overall, your memory will be more accurate, and you will get a better grade in the test.

1

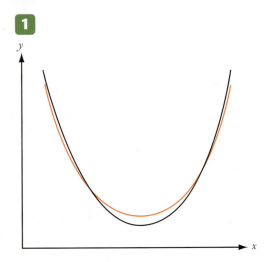

Fig. 1: *first results*

2

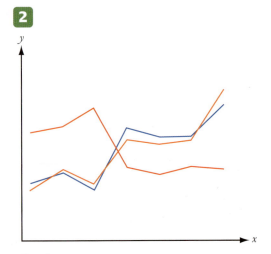

Fig. 6

3

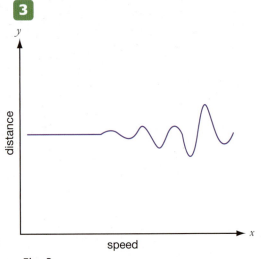

Fig. 3

4

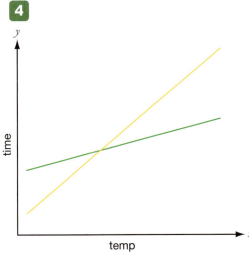

Graph of temperature against time

Theme 2

Friends and family

- Parents, Adults and Children

Friends and family

2.1 Vocabulary for reading   Stimulus and response

A   Reviewing vocabulary

All the words below are people. What is the full word in each case?

1. friend
2. coll
3. nei
4. acq
5. rel
6. ado

B   Identifying part of speech in context

Write *n* (noun) or *v* (verb) next to each word in *italics*.

1. In some cultures, people usually make a *promise* after apologizing.
2. Some people say that you shouldn't accept *blame* after a car accident.
3. Bergman and Kasper *support* the theory that apologizing is culturally determined.
4. Several pieces of research *point* to the same conclusion.
5. In some cultures, it is not polite to *excuse* your behaviour.
6. Three kinds of memory are kept in the long-term *store*.

C   Understanding new words in context

Complete the text below with a word from the right in each space. Make any necessary changes.

> Relationships with other people are never simple. _Parents_ often have problems with their children. Young children usually _____ their parents but adolescents often _____. Husbands often say 'My _____ doesn't understand me.' _____ have problems with each other.
>
> We can often understand the issues between two people by analyzing the verbal _____. In other words, we study their conversations. A lot of conversations have the form of stimulus–_____. In other words, one person says something – the _____ – and the other person _____. Sometimes, the response is expected. We know the person will reply in that way. But sometimes, it is _____. An unexpected response may reveal a problem with the relationship.

They're just inside the front door.
(expected response)

Where are my black shoes?
(stimulus)

Why don't you ever put things away?
(unexpected response)

Fig. 1: *Stimulus and responses*

arise (v)
caption (n)
contribution (n)
difficulties appear
do what you are told
feel good about
found (v)
grow up (v)
husband (n)
inferior (adj)
look after (v)
obey (v)
parent (n)
practise [= medicine]
psychiatric
psychiatry (n)
psychoanalysis (n)
psychoanalyst (n)
rebel (n and v)
reflect (v) [= show]
respond (v)
response (n)
see the point of
   (doing) something
stimulus (n)
switch (v)
take over (v)
transaction (n)
(un)expected (adj)
value (v)
wife (n)
workmate (n)

A   **Activating ideas**

Read the title of the article on the opposite page.

1. What is strange about the title?
2. What do you think the article is going to be about?

B   **Using illustrations to predict content**

Look at Figure 1. Are these statements true (T) or false (F)?

1. The husband gives the stimulus and a child gives the response.
2. The stimulus is a statement by the husband.
3. In the caption, P stands for Parent and C stands for Child.
4. A transaction in this case is a stimulus and a response.
5. The article will be about transactions between children.

C   **Using topic sentences to predict content**

1. Read the topic sentences from the article. In which paragraph do you expect to find …
    a. more explanation of the illustration? ☐
    b. more information about Berne's model of behaviour between people? ☐
    c. more information about problems with transactions? ☐
    d. more information about Berne's idea? ☐
    e. more information about Berne's life? ☐

2. Look quickly at each paragraph and check your answers.

D   **Understanding the text**

Read the sentences. Find information in the text opposite to complete each sentence.

1. Eric Berne was from Montreal.
2. He first practised psychiatry in _____.
3. Berne developed his ideas in _____.
4. Berne believed that personal problems come from _____.
5. Berne thought that you sometimes feel good because _____.
6. Berne said that people can behave like _____.
7. Berne believed that people can switch _____.
8. Berne said that problems arise if _____.

E   **Transferring information to the real world**

Analyze the transactions below. Mark each sentence P (Parent), A (Adult) or C (Child).

1.

W: You can't go out in that shirt. I'll iron another one for you. = P

H: Thanks. I don't know what I'd do without you. = C

2.

H: What shall we do this evening?

W: Let's go to a restaurant.

3.

H: I don't know what to wear.

W: I've put some clothes out for you.

4.

W: Where shall we go at the weekend?

H: Why do I have to make all the decisions?

Are you a Parent, an Adult or a Child?

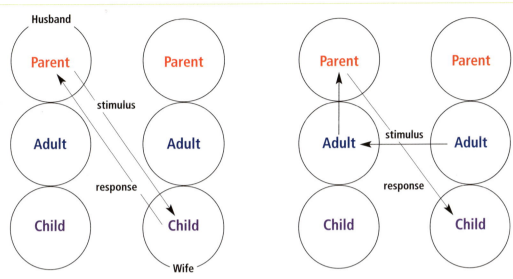

Fig. 1: *An example P–C transaction*

Fig. 2: *An example mixed transaction*

(1) Eric Berne was born in 1910 in Montreal, Canada. He moved to New York to train as a psychiatrist in the 1930s. After practising psychiatry in that city, he joined the Army Medical Corps in 1943. There was a strong demand for psychiatrists during the Second World War. At the end of the war, Berne moved to San Francisco. There, he developed a new idea about psychiatric problems. In 1964, he wrote a book called *The Games People Play*. He founded a school (or type) of psychiatry called Transactional Analysis. He died in California in 1970.

(2) In his 1964 book, Berne stated that people have problems in their life because of their relationships with other people. Before Berne made this statement, most psychiatrists believed that all personal problems came from inside the person's head. In other words, problems came from a person's own brain. However, Berne believed that problems arise because of the transactions – or conversations – between people. He pointed out that people often play games with their friends, family and workmates. By making the other person feel worse, they try to feel better about themselves. Nowadays, psychiatrists accept that people play these games.

(3) Berne developed a simple model of the behaviour between people. He said that people always behave in one of three ways. They act as a Parent (P), as an Adult (A) or as a Child (C). He explained that a Parent can try to look after another person, or try to control him/her. A Child can obey orders and do what he/she is told, or rebel.

(4) We can see an example of a P–C transaction in Figure 1. As you can see in this case, the husband behaves as a Parent and the wife behaves as the Child. For example, the husband might say 'Why did you spend so much money last month?' and the wife might respond 'I'm sorry. It won't happen again.' However, the same husband and wife could change roles in a different transaction. According to Berne, people can play roles in this way for years without any problems.

(5) However, problems often arise in transactions. For example, difficulties appear if both people in a transaction want to be the Parent or both people want to be the Child. Problems also arise if one person wants to behave like an Adult and the other person responds as a Parent or a Child. For example, in Figure 2, perhaps the wife says 'I've got to get some new shoes for the children,' and the husband replies 'Why do you spend so much money?'

A Reviewing vocabulary

Match the verbs and the other words to make phrases from the article in Lesson 2.2.

1. train   ☐ a new idea
2. practise   ☐ a role
3. obey   ☐ a school
4. join   ☐1 as a psychiatrist
5. develop   ☐ like an adult
6. found   ☐ psychiatry
7. play   ☐ the army
8. behave   ☐ an order

B Identifying a new skill

1. Read the Skills Check. How do we know in English that a sentence contains an opinion?

2. These statements are from the article in Lesson 2.2. Mark each one ✓ for fact or *?* for theory.

   a. ☐ Berne founded a school of psychiatry.
   b. ☐ Berne moved to San Francisco.
   c. ☐ People always behave in one of three ways.
   d. ☐ Berne died in California in 1970.
   e. ☐ People often play games with their friends, family and workmates.
   f. ☐ People try to feel better by making other people feel worse.
   g. ☐ There was a strong demand for psychiatrists during the Second World War.

C Practising a new skill

Identify the theories in this text. Underline them and mark with *?*.

Eric Berne wrote eight major books in his lifetime but the most famous is *Games People Play*, which he published in 1964. In this book, Berne said that people <u>behave in one of three ways in all transactions.</u> *?* Berne grew up in Canada although his family were from Eastern Europe. Berne's father was a doctor, and some people say that Berne's mother encouraged Eric to study medicine. He trained as a doctor and surgeon, then moved into the field of psychiatry. He applied to become a registered psychoanalyst in 1956 but his application was rejected. Many people believe that this rejection affected him deeply. As a result, he started to develop his own theories of psychoanalysis.

Skills Check

Fact … or theory?

Articles often contain statements of **fact**.

Examples:

*Berne was **born** in 1910.
He **joined** the Army Medical Corps in 1943.*

Articles also often contain **theories**.

Examples:

***Berne stated** that people have problems in their lives because of their relationships with other people.
He said that people always behave in one of three ways.*

Look for **introductory verbs**:
say, state, explain, point out, believe, think, feel, claim, maintain

Look also for **phrases**:
*According to (Berne), …
For (Berne), …
In (Berne's) opinion, …*

Sometimes there is **no introductory** verb or phrase. You have to decide if the statement is **fact** or **theory** from context.
They act as a Parent (P), as an Adult (A) or as a Child (C).

= theory   – part of Berne's theory

Problems came from a person's own brain.
= theory   – the view of psychiatrists before Berne's theory

Remember! Theories may be true or false.

Writers often begin sentences with a **prepositional phrase**. The prepositional phrase sometimes ends ②
with a **comma**. The **subject** of the sentence comes next. If there is no comma, try to find the end of the
prepositional phrase.

	prepositional phrase	comma	subject	verb	
After	practising psychiatry in that city		he	joined	
Before	Berne made this statement		most psychiatrists	believed	
At	the end of the war	(,)	Berne	moved	...
By	making the other person feel worse		they	try	
As	you can see in this case		the husband	is	
According	to Berne		people	can play	

A   Finding subject and verb in long sentences

There is no comma at the end of the prepositional phrases in these sentences.
Underline the subject. Circle the verb.

1. On 10th May 1910 Eric Berne was born in Montreal.
2. At the age of 18 Berne entered McGill University.
3. During his time at university he wrote for several student newspapers.
4. After graduating from university Berne started to study Psychiatry at Yale.
5. At the university at that time the professor was Dr Paul Federn.
6. At the end of his training in 1938 Berne became an American citizen.
7. During Berne's training in psychiatry the Second World War started.
8. As a result of the mental problems of soldiers during the war a large number of psychiatrists were needed by the army at that time.
9. At the end of the war in 1945 Berne went to study in San Francisco.
10. At that time in the San Francisco Psychoanalytic Institute Erik Erikson was the director.

Sometimes statements of theory are introduced. Always look closely at the tense in the introduction and ③
in the statement.

introduction		statement
Psychiatrists accept		people play these games.
Most psychiatrists believed	(that)	all personal problems came from inside the person's head.
Berne thought		problems arise because of the transactions between people.

Introduction in present = person still alive OR idea still accepted
Introduction in past = person dead OR idea no longer accepted
Statement in present = theory still accepted
Statement in past = theory no longer accepted

B   Identifying present and past theories

Read each sentence. What is the theory in each case? Is it true / possibly true or old / false?

1. People believed that the Earth was flat. = 'The Earth is flat.' = old / false
2. Aristotle believed that earthquakes were caused by winds under the earth.
3. Aristotle thought that we learn by doing.
4. Piaget said that children go through four stages.
5. Pavlov stated that you can make people behave in particular ways.
6. Al Gore says that man is the cause of global warming.

A Reviewing vocabulary

Study each sentence. What does the word in **bold** mean in both cases?

1. He **trained** to be a **train** driver.
   trained = studied, train = transport method
2. She **played** Ophelia in the **play** Hamlet.
3. He **found** the school that Berne **founded**.
4. Berne's **school** of psychiatry did not have a **school** building.
5. The lecturer **pointed** out several important **points**.
6. She **demanded** to know the **demand** for psychiatrists.
7. The **rebel** didn't like the government policies so he **rebelled**.
8. The judge didn't even **try** to **try** the men in a fair way.

B Activating ideas

Which of these statements do you agree with? Tick one.

1. ☐ I do a good job most of the time. The people around me do a good job, too.
2. ☐ I do a good job most of the time but the people around me don't.
3. ☐ I don't do a good job most of the time but the people around me do.
4. ☐ I think everyone does a poor job most of the time, including me.

C Understanding a text

1. Read the article. Mark sentences F (fact) or O (opinion) as you read.
2. Answer the questions.
   a. Where did Harris train in psychiatry? *Washington*
   b. Where did he practise psychiatry?
   c. What were the connections between Harris and Berne?
   d. What is the name of the model discussed in this article?
   e. What did some people believe before Berne's theory?
   f. Which type of relationship do people have when they are young?
   g. What sometimes happens as people grow up?
   h. Why is Relationship Type 1 healthy?
   i. How did Harris feel about the other types of relationship?
   j. How can you move from the other types to Type 1?

D Transferring information to real-world situations

Match the statements below to each type of relationship, 1 to 4.

A *We're really getting on well with this.*

C *Why am I so useless? You have to do everything for me.*

B *Let's give up. It's hopeless. We'll never be able to do it.*

D *Here. Give it to me. I'll do it.*

E Developing critical thinking

Do you recognize yourself or another person in the descriptions of relationship types? Explain your answer.

I'm OK, you're OK

(1) Thomas Harris was born in California, USA in 1910. After graduating in Medicine from the University of Arkansas, he moved to Washington D.C. There, he began his training in psychiatry in 1942. At the end of his studies, he joined the Navy, where he practised psychiatry for several years. Then he left to take up a teaching post at his old university. He worked with Eric Berne and, in 1969, published *I'm OK, You're OK*, which developed one of Berne's ideas. After moving back to California, he took over from Berne as the director of the Transactional Analysis Society. He died in 1995.

(2) Before Berne's theory, some psychiatrists believed that people were born with particular attitudes towards other people. However, Berne believed that everyone is born OK. At the time of their birth, babies feel good about themselves and about other people. Other people are OK, too. These relationships are Type 1 – see Figure 1.

(3) However, as they grow up, Harris thought that people may change. As we can see in Figure 1, three other relationships are possible. According to Harris, people may move to any of the other three boxes. He pointed out that nobody has exactly the same relationship with everybody all of the time, but for most of the time, their relationships reflect that attitude to themselves and other people.

(4) For Harris, only Relationship 1 is a healthy one. In this kind of relationship, people are happy to work with other people. They respect the contribution of another person, but they are also confident in their own contribution.

(5) There are problems in the other three cases. In Relationship 2, a person does not respect other people or their contribution to work. In the third relationship, a person feels stupid and inferior to other people, while in the final relationship, a person does not see the point of doing anything.

(6) Harris believed that there is hope for people with bad attitudes. In other words, the positions are not fixed. If you recognize that you do not value other people, you can try to find things to value in them. Then you can try to move to Relationship 1. If you recognize that you do not value *yourself*, make a list of good things about yourself and try to accept that you are OK. If you think everyone is hopeless, do both the points above.

		you	
		OK	not OK
me	OK	relationship type 1	relationship type 2
	not OK	relationship type 3	relationship type 4

Figure 1: *The I'm OK, you're OK model*

Theme 3

Managing to be successful

- Decisions, decisions, decisions

Managing to be successful

3.1 Vocabulary for reading   The language of problems and solutions

A   Reviewing vocabulary

Find pairs of opposites in the box.

Example: *attend – miss*

attend	calm	stressed	confident
doubtful	current	previous	either
neither	refuse	agree	remember
forget	miss	ugly	beautiful
waste	use	work	rest

B   Predicting prepositions in context

What is the missing preposition in each sentence?

1. People sometimes don't approve *of* _____ the actions of a friend.
2. The scientist thought _____ a possible solution.
3. Let's go back _____ the first problem.
4. How can we deal _____ this issue?
5. Let's work _____ an example.
6. The researchers had to come up _____ another idea.
7. If you are sure that you are right, you should stick _____ your opinion.
8. Many people agree _____ this point of view.
9. People sometimes make fun _____ new ideas.
10. A manager needs someone to rely _____ inside the organization.

C   Understanding new words

Read each sentence below. Study the underlined word in each case. It is built from a word that you **know already**. What is that word in each case?

1. The manager found it difficult to make <u>decisions</u>. *decide*
2. We can <u>define</u> the word *style* in a number of ways. _____
3. You need to <u>evaluate</u> each solution carefully. _____
4. It is easy to <u>identify</u> the cause of the problem. _____
5. People in <u>management</u> are responsible for many problems inside companies. _____
6. The students have a <u>participatory</u> role in the process. _____
7. There is a small <u>possibility</u> of finding a peaceful solution. _____
8. In <u>reality</u>, the people would never accept this answer. _____
9. There is a <u>saying</u> in English: 'Measure three times, cut once.' _____
10. I would like to <u>summarize</u> the main issues in this essay. _____

acronym *(n)*
approach *(n)* [= method]
at the same time
autocrat *(n)*
come up with *(v)*
cross *(n)*
decide *(v)*
define *(v)*
democrat *(n)*
do the right thing
evaluate *(v)*
generate *(v)*
hire *(v)*
identify *(v)*
imagine *(v)*
in reality
instinct *(n)*
logical *(adj)*
management *(n)*
management style
obvious *(adj)*
participatory *(adj)*
perfect *(adj)*
possibility *(n)*
public transport
retain *(v)*
saying *(n)*
stick to *(v)* [= keep]
summarize
take *(v)* [= get/catch]
without thinking
work through *(v)*
worker *(n)*

_____
_____
_____

3.2 Real-time reading   'Digest' problems to make good decisions

A   Activating ideas

Discuss in groups.

1. What was the last big decision you made?
2. How did you make the decision?
3. Do you regret the decision now?

B   Understanding paragraph structure

Cover the article opposite. Read the topic sentences from the article. Match each topic sentence with the next sentence in the paragraph. Then uncover the article and check.

1. How do you make decisions?

2. We can summarize the process of good decision-making in the acronym DIGEST.

3. Firstly, **define** the problem – say what you are really trying to do.

4. Let's work through an example of the process in action.

5. You will not make perfect decisions every time, even with this decision-making process.

☐ However, there is an old saying in business …

☐ First, the problem.

☐ What does DIGEST mean?

☐ A lot of the time people make decisions without really thinking about it.

☐ Secondly, **imagine** a successful solution.

C   Understanding the text

Read the article. Mark each sentence T (true), F (false) or not certain (?).

1. ☐ Using *instinct* means not really thinking about something.
2. ☐ Good decision-making only really matters in business.
3. ☐ DIGEST is the acronym for a decision-making process.
4. ☐ The writer has chosen the acronym because *digest* means 'to break down food in the stomach'.
5. ☐ *Generate alternative solutions* means 'think of different answers to the problem'.
6. ☐ The writer thinks you should involve other people in generating alternatives.
7. ☐ You should evaluate each solution as you think of it.
8. ☐ The creative side of the brain is the left side.
9. ☐ The last stage of the process is selecting the best solution.
10. ☐ The writer thinks it is better not to make a decision than to make a bad one.

D   Developing critical thinking

Think about the example situation from this article (paragraph 4).
Go through the DIGEST process in pairs. Tell the other pairs your decision.

'Digest' problems to make good decisions
It's the process that matters

How do you make decisions? A lot of the time people make decisions without really thinking about it. They use their instinct, and just hope that they have done the right thing. However, this kind of decision-making is no good in business, and probably not the best way to decide big things in our everyday lives either. If you follow the process carefully, the decision will usually be a good one.

We can summarize the process of good decision-making in the acronym DIGEST. What does DIGEST mean? In general English, it has a number of meanings, including 'to break down food in the stomach', but, in this case, the word just helps us remember the six parts of the process.

Firstly, **define** the problem – say what you are really trying to do. Secondly, **imagine** a successful solution. This is usually easy. (If it isn't, go back to the first stage again and re-define the problem.) Thirdly, **generate** alternative possibilities. There is very rarely only one possible solution to a problem. Think of several solutions and you are more likely to come up with a good one in the end. Fourthly, **evaluate** the possibilities – look at each one carefully and consider the good and the bad points about it. Fifthly, **select** the best one. (Again, an obvious stage.) Finally, **tell** people your decision. You should certainly do this if the decision affects other people. Even if it doesn't, you should tell other people because it might be difficult to stick to your decision later. The more people you *tell* about your decision, the harder it is to change your mind later.

Table 1: *The DIGEST process*

D_{efine}	the problem
I_{magine}	a successful solution
G_{enerate}	alternative possibilities
E_{valuate}	the possibilities
S_{elect}	the best one
T_{ell}	people your decision

Let's work through an example of the process in action. First, the problem. Let's say that you have lectures every morning and keep arriving late. You imagine a successful solution to the problem. That is easy in this case. You need to arrive ten minutes before the first lecture. However, perhaps you live a long way from the university and the first lecture begins at 9.00. You need to generate some alternative possibilities. You could take a bus, but don't like public transport … Stop! During the brainstorm, you must not evaluate the possibilities or criticize them. Why? Because there are two sides to the human brain – a creative side, and a logical side. It is impossible to get both sides working well at the same time. In this case, you need the creative side first, to generate the alternatives, then the logical side, to evaluate each one. So, make a list of possibilities. You could take a taxi, or go in your father's car. You could hire a driver, or stay overnight with a friend, etc. Then go through them one by one, thinking of any difficulties. You could give each possibility a number of crosses, one for each difficulty. Finally, when you have evaluated all the possibilities, you need to select one. And that's it. Well, not quite. Tell people about it, remember.

You will not make perfect decisions every time, even with this decision-making process. However, there is an old saying in business: 'There is only one thing worse than a bad decision and that is no decision at all.'

A Reviewing vocabulary

Complete each part of the DIGEST approach.

1. Define   *the problem.*
2. Imagine ....
3. Generate ....
4. Evaluate ....
5. Select   ....
6. Tell   ....

B Identifying a new skill

1. Read the Skills Check. What are non-text markers?

2. Look at the highlighted sections in the text in Lesson 3.2. Find the non-text markers. What is each marker, and what is its purpose?

Example:

<mark>What does DIGEST mean?</mark>

DIGEST = acronym. It stands for the mnemonic Define, Imagine, etc.

C Practising a new skill (1)

What is each acronym?

Example: *WHO is an organization.*

WHO	UN	NASA	EU	UK	USA	MBA
SMS	BBC	PC	ISP	CEO		

D Practising a new skill (2)

Complete sentences 1–6 with the endings below.

1 There is a style of management called MBO ...

2 It is based on the saying ...

3 If a worker knows the objective of a job, his/her decision will be as good as the manager's, ...

4 In MBO, managers set the objectives but decisions are made by everyone – ...

5 The key to successful MBO is giving workers ...

6 If managers don't really give power away, MBO will not work ...

☐ and may damage the relationship between workers and managers.

☐ 'Give a person a map, not a route.'

☐ (Management By Objectives).

☐ it is called *delegation*.

☐ perhaps better.

☐ power.

Skills Check

Understanding non-text markers

There are sometimes marks in a text which tell you something important about information.

Here are some of the most common ones with their usual meanings.

marker	name	meaning
(word)	brackets	extra information
– word	dash	next information is a definition OR an example
'word' OR "word"	speech marks	actual speech OR something that people say OR a definition OR unusual use of a word
word	italics	the information is important
word	bold	the information is important
WORD	acronym	the name of an organization or idea
word ...	suspension dots	this sentence is not complete

When writers join two sentences with *and*, *but*, *or*, they sometimes omit words from the second sentence. ④

sentence 1		sentence 2
People use their instinct.	and	~~They~~ hope that they have done the right thing.
You have lectures every morning.	and	~~You~~ keep arriving late.
The lecturer does not know.	or	~~The lecturer does not~~ care about your problems.
You could take a taxi.	or	~~You could~~ go in your father's car.
Decision-making is not a moment in time.	but	~~Decision-making is~~ a process.
During the brainstorming of ideas, you must not evaluate.	or	~~You must not~~ criticize them.

Always think: *What is the subject (and verb) of this part of the sentence? Is it negative?*

A   Identifying missing subjects

Find the second verb in each sentence. What is the subject in each case? Is the verb negative?

1.   Perhaps you have lectures every morning and / keep arriving late.   *you*

2.   Thomas Harris was born in California but studied Medicine at the University of Arkansas.

3.   People are often happy to work in groups and respect the contributions of other people.

4.   Most children do not make many decisions inside a family but accept the decisions of parents.

5.   Adolescents sometimes don't accept their parents' decision and rebel.

6.   Every moment, we pay attention to sensory memories or ignore them.

7.   Loftus and Palmer showed students a film and asked them to complete a questionnaire about it.

8.   Charles Dickens, the English novelist, left school at 12 and went to work in a factory.

9.   Mobile phones are very useful but can also waste a lot of time.

10.   The aural learner does not respond well to written information but learns from lectures and tutorials.

B   Identifying the missing subject and modal auxiliary

Find the second verb in each sentence. What is the subject and modal auxiliary in each case?

1.   Managers have to communicate their ideas and ensure that workers understand them.   *Managers have to*

2.   Directors should provide regular and full information and keep workers up-to-date.

3.   In order to remember information, you must take it out of memory and use it again and again.

4.   Humans cannot remember every event in their lives or name all their childhood friends.

5.   Doctors in the past could not treat many diseases or save people from fatal infections.

6.   In this report, I am going to discuss the reasons for the problem and suggest possible solutions.

7.   Soon, the world will not have enough oil for global needs or have enough renewable energy sources to meet demand.

8.   People may not be able to use cars or travel by air as much as today.

A   Reviewing vocabulary

Find a word to complete each phrase.

1. the right   ☐ one
2. everyday   ☐ say
3. an old   ☐ brain
4. the human   ☐ thinking
5. let's   ☐ thing
6. at the same ☐ saying
7. one by   ☐ lives
8. without   ☐ time

B   Activating ideas

Read the title of the article on the opposite page.

1. How would you answer the question?

2. What will the article tell you, in general terms?

C   Understanding a text

Read each paragraph. Do the activities below.

para 1 1. What is management style?
        2. Find examples of non-text markers in paragraph 1. Why has the writer used each marker?
para 2 What do the *workers* do in each style of management?
para 3 Follow the instructions in the paragraph. What is *your* management style? Explain your answer.
para 4 Follow the instructions in the paragraph. What do your friends say?
para 5 Why might an autocratic manager change his/her style at home?

D   Developing critical thinking

What are the advantages in *business* of each management style?

1. autocratic

2. participatory

3. democratic

stages	me	them
D		
I		
G		
E		
S		
T		

E   Developing vocabulary

1. In the article, what word was used after each verb on the right?

   Example: miss the point

2. What other words are commonly used with these verbs?

   Examples: miss the bus, miss my family

miss	the point
make	
retain	
achieve	
change	
involve	
organize	
manage	

Are you an autocrat or a democrat?

It's all a matter of style

What is your management style? If you say 'I have no idea, I'm not a manager', you are missing the point. In the first place, we are all managers of our daily lives. In the second place, we all have a normal management *style*, whether or not we have a management *job*. Your management style is the way you deal with people, particularly when you have to make decisions which involve other people. It is very important to know your style, because you may be using the wrong style at times to achieve your objectives. As you know, a good approach to decision-making is the DIGEST system (see *Digest ...* in this publication). We can reveal a person's management style by asking this question: 'When do you involve workers in a decision?'

The old style of management in business was autocratic. In an *autocratic* style, the manager does not ask for any help or involve the workers at any stage in the process (see Table 1). However, nowadays, many managers use a *participatory* management style. They involve the workers in some stages but retain control of the decision-making (see Table 2). In a third style, called *democratic* – Table 3 – the manager involves the workers at all stages except defining the problem (D) and telling people the decision (T). This style is still unusual in business.

So what is *your* management style? Imagine that you have to make a decision which involves other people. For example, let's say that your tutor has asked you to organize a social event for the students in your group. You could make all the decisions yourself or ask the other students to help you at any stage. Draw up a table (like 1, 2 and 3 on the right) and put ticks against each part of DIGEST.

Now show your table to your friends, because the views of other people are very important in a case like this. They may agree with your ticks or think that you have not been honest about your *real* management style. You may think, for example, that you involve people in generating alternative possibilities. But in reality, you will only accept your *own* possibilities and make fun of any other suggestions.

So what is your *real* management style – autocratic, participatory or democratic? Once you know your management style, you can make another decision. You can decide to change your style completely or for particular situations. For example, an autocratic manager at *work* may not 'manage' his wife or her husband in this way, or a teenage child.

Table 1: *Autocratic management*

stages	manager	workers
D	✓	
I	✓	
G	✓	
E	✓	
S	✓	
T	✓	

Table 2: *Participatory management*

stages	manager	workers
D	✓	
I	✓	
G	✓	✓
E	✓	✓
S	✓	
T	✓	

Table 3: *Democratic management*

stages	manager	workers
D	✓	
I	✓	✓
G	✓	✓
E	✓	✓
S	✓	✓
T	✓	

Theme 4

Natural cycles

- Chains, webs and pyramids

Natural cycles

4.1 Vocabulary for reading   Climate areas

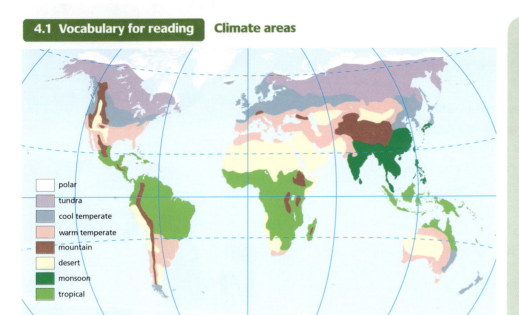

- polar
- tundra
- cool temperate
- warm temperate
- mountain
- desert
- monsoon
- tropical

Figure 1: *World climate areas (worldclimate.com)*

A **Understanding world maps**

1. Label Figure 1 with the words from the box.
2. What do the different colours indicate?
3. What colour is your country?
4. What does that colour mean?

Equator	Tropic of Cancer
Tropic of Capricorn	
North Pole	South Pole

B **Understanding new words in context**

Read the encyclopedia entries below. Copy a climate name from Figure 1 into each space.

desert — An area with less than 25 cm of rain a year. These areas have hot days and cold nights.

_____ — An area near the North Pole or the South Pole with a maximum temperature of 10°C.

_____ — An area with generally mild summers and mild winters but there can be extremes of temperature. These areas are divided into cool and warm.

_____ — An area normally between latitude 10 degrees north and 20 degrees south of the Equator. These climates have an average temperature around 25°C and at least 150 cm of rain a year.

_____ — An area near the North Pole with no trees. The area under the surface of the earth is permanently frozen.

_____ — A tropical area with very high rainfall in the summer season.

_____ — An area of very high land with cold winters and mild summers.

C **Developing critical thinking**

1. Which climate area do you live in?
2. Do you agree with the climate description in Exercise B for your area?

carnivore *(n)*
chemical energy
consumer (animal)
convert *(v)*
desert (climate)
destroy *(v)*
ecology *(n)*
ecosystem *(n)*
endangered *(adj)*
environment *(n)*
Equator
extant *(adj)*
extinct *(adj)*
food chain
food pyramid
food web
habitat *(n)*
heat energy
herbivore *(n)*
in the first place
omnivore *(n)*
organism *(n)*
photosynthesis *(n)*
polar (climate)
process *(n)*
producer (plant)
solar energy
survive *(v)*
temperate (climate)
transfer *(v)*
tropical (climate)

A **Activating ideas**

1. What does each photograph on the right show?
2. How many links are there in each photograph?
3. How do we use the words *chain* and *web* in everyday life?

B **Understanding text organization**

Scan the text on the opposite page.

1. How is the text organized?
2. Where can you find this kind of text?
3. What does the sign ⇒ mean?

C **Preparing to read**

Write some research questions to prepare for this lecture.

School of Biological Sciences
Lecture 3

In this lecture, we look at *ecology* and we see the difference between an *environment* and an *ecosystem*. We also examine some of the relationships between living things.

Figure 1: _____

D **Understanding the text**

1. Use the highlighted parts of the science encyclopedia opposite to find answers to your research questions in Exercise C. Follow any links.
2. Write a caption for each figure on the right.
3. What are some of the relationships between the living things in the figures?

lion   dog

giraffe

impala   zebra   wildebeest

tree   grass

E **Understanding vocabulary in context**

Find a verb in the highlighted entries for each definition.

1. convert	change from one state to another
2.	continue to live, not die
3.	move from one place to another
4.	help, assist, enable to exist
5.	damage so repair is not possible
6.	take away

Figure 2: _____

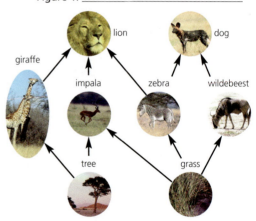

F **Developing critical thinking**

Look at the pictures below Figure 2.

1. Draw arrows to show the links between the items.
2. What will happen to this food chain if:
   - fishermen catch all the fish?
   - sealers kill all the seals?
   - the ocean water gets too warm for the plankton to survive?

ecology	The study of the relationship between living things and their ⇒**environment**. We learn from ecology that livings things depend on each other to survive. This is because all living things are involved in ⇒**food chains** and ⇒**food webs**.
ecosystem	All the animals and plants which live in a particular area, and the relationship between them. An ecosystem supports the animals and plants but a change in the ⇒**environment** may destroy an ecosystem, e.g., the advance of a ⇒**desert** may destroy a grassland. People can change or destroy an ecosystem as well, e.g., by building towns in green areas.
emigration	Movement of an ⇒**organism** from one location to another, often as a result of a change in the ⇒**ecosystem**.
endangered	An animal or plant which is close to becoming ⇒**extinct**.
energy	The power which enables us to do work. All energy comes from the Sun in the first place. Some plants convert the Sun's energy into chemical energy. They are the first link in every ⇒**food chain**.
environment (an)	A place which has a particular ⇒**climate** and landscape. There are a number of major environments on Earth, e.g., ⇒**desert**, the ⇒**tropics**.
extant	An animal or plant which is still alive and ⇒**reproducing**. All species currently alive on earth are extant (opposite: ⇒**extinct**).
extinct	An animal or plant which is no longer living on Earth (opposite: ⇒**extant**). Species often become extinct because of changes in the ⇒**ecosystem**.
flow-through system	A system with an input and an output of ⇒**energy**. For example, a ⇒**food chain** is a flow-through system with some of the energy consumed by the animal at every stage.
food chain	This is the way in which ⇒**energy** is transferred from one living thing to another. At the top of every food chain, there is an animal which eats other animals. At the bottom of every food chain, there is a plant which can convert the Sun's ⇒**energy** into food. If we remove one part of a food chain, there will be a reaction in another part of the chain.
food value	The relative amount of ⇒**nutrition** which is obtained from a particular food.
food web	This is a connection of two or more ⇒**food chains**. It shows relationships between the animals and plants in a certain ⇒**ecosystem**. Most animals and plants are part of a food web with 10, 20 or 30 other living things. This means it is very difficult in real life to predict the effect of a change in one part of the web.
Gaia	This is an idea which was put forward by ⇒**James Lovelock**. It suggests that all living things are part of one mass which can change its ⇒**environment** to ensure its survival. This is not necessarily good news for human beings. Gaia might change the Earth in a way that makes it unfit for humans.

A   Reviewing vocabulary

Which preposition do you expect to follow each verb phrase or noun phrase below?

1. depend   on
2. be involved   ....
3. come   ....
4. convert   ....
5. transfer   ....
6. be part   ....
7. learn   ....
8. the relationship   ....
9. the connection   ....
10. the effect   ....

B   Identifying a new skill

Read the Skills Check. Then decide if each statement is true (T) or false (F).

1. ☐ Some useful encyclopedias are on the Internet.
2. ☐ Research questions give you a purpose for reading.
3. ☐ You need to read a complete entry in an encyclopedia to understand it properly.
4. ☐ Links in an online encyclopedia are usually in red type.
5. ☐ It is easy to lose your way in an encyclopedia.
6. ☐ The Back button does not work with an online encyclopedia.

C   Practising a new skill

Look again at the text on page 41.

Study each research question below. Then make a list of the linked entries in each case.

research questions	links
1. What is a flow-through system?	energy, food chain
2. What is food value?	
3. What is an endangered animal or plant?	
4. What is Gaia?	
5. What is emigration in ecology?	

D   Understanding a text

Answer the research questions in Exercise C above. Only follow relevant links.

Skills Check

Using encyclopedias

Encyclopedias are a very good source for research. They can be **printed books** or on the **Internet**. But you can waste a lot of time reading information in encyclopedias which is not useful to you.

1. Always read an encyclopedia entry **for a purpose**. Write research questions before you look at the encyclopedia, e.g., *What is ecology?* *What is a food chain?*

2. **Do not read** the whole of a long entry. Stop when you have answers to your research questions.

3. Make a note of links to extra information, e.g., ⇒**ecosystem** or *ecosystem*.

4. Follow useful links. But be careful! Some links may not be useful. Think: *Will the link help me answer the research question(s)?*

5. Put a **marker** in each page of a printed encyclopedia before you go to another entry. If you don't do this, it may take you a long time to find the important entries again.

6. Click the **Back** button to return to the original page after reading each entry in an Internet encyclopedia. If you don't do this, you may lose your way in all the links.

Adding information with *which / that*

Writers often give more information about a complement with *which* or *that*. ⑤

S	V	C		V	extra information
Energy	is	the power		enables	us to do work.
Ecosystems	are	areas	which / that	have	a particular climate.
Gaia	is	an idea		was put forward	by James Lovelock.

which / that replaces the subject of the second verb.

S	V	C	S	V	extra information
Energy	is	the power.	The power	enables	us to do work.
Ecosystems	are	areas.	The areas	have	a particular climate.
Gaia	is	an idea.	The idea	was put forward	by James Lovelock.

Make sure you understand the general noun in the complement before you read the *which / that* section of the sentence.

A Understanding the general noun

Choose a general noun from the box to match the subject of each sentence.

| a chemical   an animal   an area   ~~a theory~~   a plant   a process   a subject   a machine |
| a vehicle   a gas |

1. Learning by doing is   *a theory*_____   which was proposed by Aristotle.
2. Condensation is   ....   which converts water vapour into water.
3. A jungle is   ....   which has a large number of tropical trees.
4. Carbon dioxide is   ....   which prevents heat energy from escaping into Space.
5. A tram is   ....   which runs along grooves in the road.
6. A mammal is   ....   which gives birth to live young.
7. A decomposer is   ....   which breaks down dead animals or plants into chemicals.
8. Media Studies is   ....   which looks at the mass media, like television and the Internet.
9. A nitrate is   ....   which helps plants to grow.
10. A generator is   ....   which makes electricity.

B Predicting extra information after *which*

What information do you expect to read after each *which*?
1. An extinct plant is a plant which *does not exist on Earth any more.*..........
2. An endangered animal is an animal which ....
3. A food web is a number of food chains which ....
4. A desert is an area which ....
5. Short-term memory is the part of your brain which ....
6. A prompt in a test is something which ....
7. Transactional Analysis is an idea which ....
8. *I'm OK, You're OK* is a book which ....
9. Evaporation is a process which ....
10. The Great Man-made River is a project which ....

C Identifying *which* in context

Look again at the text in Lesson 4.2. Circle all the *which* words. What subject does each word give extra information about?

A Reviewing vocabulary

Which word or phrase from this section does each phrase define?

1. food chain _____   the way in which energy is transferred from one living thing to another
2. _____   the amount of nutrition which is obtained from a particular food
3. _____   an animal or plant which no longer exists on the Earth
4. _____   the place which a group of animals and plants live in
5. _____   a system which contains a number of food chains
6. _____   an animal or plant which still lives on the Earth
7. _____   an animal or plant which is becoming extinct
8. _____   an area which has a particular climate

B Activating ideas

Study Figure 1 on the right and read the text below.

> In the diagram, we can see part of an ecosystem. At the top of the diagram, we have a snake. This snake must eat five frogs a day. Each frog must eat three grasshoppers. The grasshoppers get energy from eating huge amounts of grass.

1. Write the names of the living things in the correct place.
2. Write the total number of each animal involved.

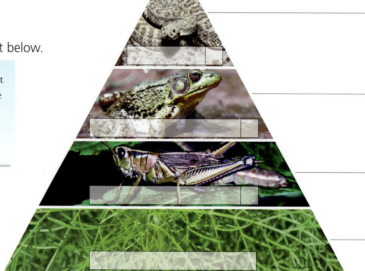

C Preparing to read

Read the lecture notice from the School of Biological Sciences. Write your research questions.

Figure 1: _____

D Understanding a text

1. Do research using the extracts from a website opposite. Make notes on the specialist terms.
2. Write a caption for Figure 1 on the right.
3. Name each level in Figure 1.

> ## School of Biological Sciences
> **Lecture 4: Ecosystems**
>
> In this lecture, we look at ways of classifying the animals and plants in an ecosystem.
>
> Research the following terms before the lecture:
> • *producers*
> • *consumers*

E Remembering key words

Define each of these words from your research. Use a sentence with *which*.

a consumer   a producer   a carnivore   a herbivore
an omnivore   a food pyramid   photosynthesis

Example: A consumer is an animal which eats a producer or another animal.

F Developing critical thinking

> ... only ten per cent of the energy is transferred from one level to the next.

What is the connection between this statement from the web encyclopedia and vegetarianism?

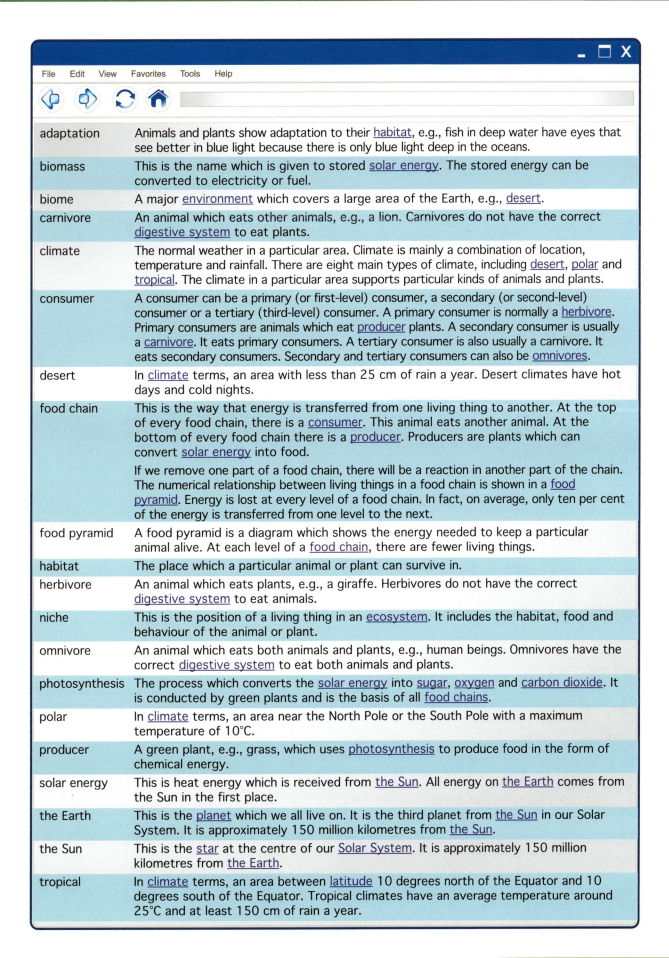

| File | Edit | View | Favorites | Tools | Help |

adaptation	Animals and plants show adaptation to their habitat, e.g., fish in deep water have eyes that see better in blue light because there is only blue light deep in the oceans.
biomass	This is the name which is given to stored solar energy. The stored energy can be converted to electricity or fuel.
biome	A major environment which covers a large area of the Earth, e.g., desert.
carnivore	An animal which eats other animals, e.g., a lion. Carnivores do not have the correct digestive system to eat plants.
climate	The normal weather in a particular area. Climate is mainly a combination of location, temperature and rainfall. There are eight main types of climate, including desert, polar and tropical. The climate in a particular area supports particular kinds of animals and plants.
consumer	A consumer can be a primary (or first-level) consumer, a secondary (or second-level) consumer or a tertiary (third-level) consumer. A primary consumer is normally a herbivore. Primary consumers are animals which eat producer plants. A secondary consumer is usually a carnivore. It eats primary consumers. A tertiary consumer is also usually a carnivore. It eats secondary consumers. Secondary and tertiary consumers can also be omnivores.
desert	In climate terms, an area with less than 25 cm of rain a year. Desert climates have hot days and cold nights.
food chain	This is the way that energy is transferred from one living thing to another. At the top of every food chain, there is a consumer. This animal eats another animal. At the bottom of every food chain there is a producer. Producers are plants which can convert solar energy into food.
	If we remove one part of a food chain, there will be a reaction in another part of the chain. The numerical relationship between living things in a food chain is shown in a food pyramid. Energy is lost at every level of a food chain. In fact, on average, only ten per cent of the energy is transferred from one level to the next.
food pyramid	A food pyramid is a diagram which shows the energy needed to keep a particular animal alive. At each level of a food chain, there are fewer living things.
habitat	The place which a particular animal or plant can survive in.
herbivore	An animal which eats plants, e.g., a giraffe. Herbivores do not have the correct digestive system to eat animals.
niche	This is the position of a living thing in an ecosystem. It includes the habitat, food and behaviour of the animal or plant.
omnivore	An animal which eats both animals and plants, e.g., human beings. Omnivores have the correct digestive system to eat both animals and plants.
photosynthesis	The process which converts the solar energy into sugar, oxygen and carbon dioxide. It is conducted by green plants and is the basis of all food chains.
polar	In climate terms, an area near the North Pole or the South Pole with a maximum temperature of 10°C.
producer	A green plant, e.g., grass, which uses photosynthesis to produce food in the form of chemical energy.
solar energy	This is heat energy which is received from the Sun. All energy on the Earth comes from the Sun in the first place.
the Earth	This is the planet which we all live on. It is the third planet from the Sun in our Solar System. It is approximately 150 million kilometres from the Sun.
the Sun	This is the star at the centre of our Solar System. It is approximately 150 million kilometres from the Earth.
tropical	In climate terms, an area between latitude 10 degrees north of the Equator and 10 degrees south of the Equator. Tropical climates have an average temperature around 25°C and at least 150 cm of rain a year.

Theme 5

Customs: origins and effects

- The price of happiness

Customs: origins and effects

5.1 Vocabulary for reading   Doing research

A Understanding vocabulary in context

Read the article from a university booklet.

1. Choose the correct form of each word in red.
2. What is the writer's view of each statement below?
   a. Information on the Internet is usually wrong.
   b. Writers on the web are always biased.
   c. It is easy to recognize bias.
   d. You often need to check several sources.

B Using new vocabulary

Discuss the questions in pairs.

1. How can you read *widely*?
2. How do you recognize a *quote* in an article?
3. Name a *popular* magazine.
4. Name an *academic* journal.
5. Is a medical journal an *authoritative* source? Why (not)?
6. How can you *validate* information?
7. What is the *bias* of most national newspapers in your country?
8. How many *extreme* adjectives can you think of?
9. What is your *view* of arranged marriages?
10. Do you have any *evidence* to *support* your view?

How to do research

When you write assignments, you have to do research, which means reading widely / wide, using a variety of source / sources, including, nowadays, the Internet. It does not mean just checking out Wikipedia and quote / quoting it word for word.

When students did all their research in the library, it was easy to find authoritative / author sources, because they could see the difference between a popular / popularity magazine and an academic journal / journals. On the web, you need to check who the writer is, who he/she is writing for, and whether the article just provides an overview or detailed / detail research.

You need to validate / valid all 'facts' on the web because many writers of web articles are bias / biased in favour of or against their topic. For example, people are often ethnocentric and think their own culture is always right. Sometimes they state / are stating their bias. They say clearly 'In my opinion / opinions ...' Sometimes, though, they are not so direct, but they use extremely / extreme words, particularly adjectives, like *stupid* and *disgusting*, or *brilliant* and *delicious*. Sometimes, they only imply / implies things – in other words, you have to work out the opinion of the writer from the kind of evidence / evidences they give.

So you must critically / critical evaluate any information you read on a website. Keep thinking: *What does the writer think about this point?* Or perhaps, more importantly: *What does the writer want **me** to think?* If the writer gives evidence in support / supporting of a particular point of views / view, you may need to find evidence *against* in another article.

affair *(n)* [= event]
afford *(v)*
arranged marriage
bias *(n)*
bridal *(adj)*
bride price
child bride
child labour
clearly *(adv)*
consequences *(n pl)*
critically *(adv)*
dowry *(n)*
economy *(n)* [= saving]
edit *(v)*
evidence *(n)*
expense/s *(n)*
extreme *(n)*
forbid *(v)*
foreigner *(n)*
gift *(n)*
hire *(v)*
illegal *(adj)*
illiteracy *(n)*
imply *(v)*
incentive *(n)*
jewellery *(n)*
journal *(n)*
loan *(n)*
national *(n)* [= person]
opinion *(n)*
pay off
popular *(adj)*
prospective *(adj)*
quote *(n)*
references *(n pl)*
sensible *(adj)*
share *(v)*
source *(n)*
specialist *(n)*
state *(n)*
support *(n)*
tool *(n)*
validate *(v)*
view *(n)*
waste *(n)*
weaken *(v)*

A Activating ideas

1. The average cost of weddings in many countries, including the USA, has risen steeply in the last 20 years. Why? Think of some possible reasons.

2. What has happened to wedding costs in your country in the same period? Why?

B Preparing to read

1. Look at the headline, photos and highlighted topic sentences. What will the main point of the article be?

2. Read the topic sentences again. What information do you expect to find in each paragraph? Write the paragraph number next to each topic.

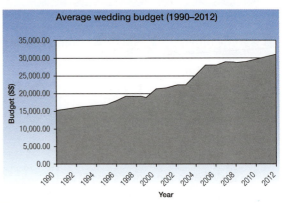

Average wedding budget (1990–2012)

weddingplanner.com

a the attempts of governments to deal with the problem	
b mass weddings	
c the cost of weddings in different countries	
d hiring wedding clothes	
e the introduction to the article	1
f quotes from young people about the cost of weddings	
g marrying a foreign bride – reasons for this and perhaps problems	

C Understanding the text

1. Read the text. Check your answers to Exercise B.

2. Find three facts and three opinions in the text.

D Understanding the main point of a text

This article is not complete. Choose the best conclusion below.

1	A wedding can be an expensive business, but with help from the government, and economies from the bride and groom, it is possible to make it affordable. All cultures have a form of marriage and it seems unlikely that cost will deter people from going ahead.
2	Weddings are becoming more and more expensive. As a result, more and more people are deciding not to get married at all. All cultures have a form of marriage but the increasing cost may eventually kill off the custom completely in some countries.

E Developing critical thinking

1. What are the main problems with weddings, according to the article?

2. What are some of the solutions in the text?

3. Can you think of any additional solutions?

F Understanding vocabulary in context

Find ten words or expressions in the text which are connected with money.

CAN COUPLES AFFORD TO GET MARRIED ANYMORE?

1 Do you want to get married in the near future? Or perhaps the question should be, can you afford to get married in the near future? All countries must deal with the rising cost of marriage in one way or another. If you do not deal with problems, they get worse.

2 In many countries in the world, weddings are becoming extremely expensive affairs, with even a relatively simple one costing more than £50,000. The money goes on the bride's wardrobe, on her jewellery and, in some cultures, on a sum paid by the groom's father to her father (called *bride price*) or from the bride's father to the groom's father (called a *dowry*). Finally, there is often a huge reception for all the friends and relatives. The expense is simply too high for many grooms and their families. If they don't have the money, they often go into debt to pay for the wedding. In some countries, 80 per cent of all personal loans are used to cover wedding expenses.

3 Young people in these countries know all about the cost of a wedding. 'When my sister got married, it was very grand,' said Huda, who is studying Graphic Design at college. 'It was a traditional wedding and it lasted three days. It was beautiful and made us very happy, but, for me, it was a waste of money. Today, when I ask my sister about the cost, she regrets it. She says, "If I had the money now, I would spend it on my child and my house."' Nabilah, a Media Studies student, nods in agreement. 'I have a cousin who got married 11 years ago and he is still paying off the debts! When I get married, I won't spend a lot of money.'

4 In some countries, men solve the problem by marrying foreign brides because the bride price is much lower. But surely that is not really a solution? If men marry out of their religion and their culture, there may not be enough nationals for the local women to marry in the future.

5 Some countries have taken extreme decisions to solve the problem, making marriages between nationals and foreigners illegal. Other countries go for the more sensible option of offering incentives. For example, nationals may get loans or gifts to nationals if they marry a local girl. These schemes seem to be very successful. In the UAE, for example, a scheme of this sort has helped 44,000 couples to get married in the last ten years.

6 Another possible economy is the mass-wedding, which is a ceremony with hundreds of brides and grooms at the same time. They can be huge affairs but all the couples share the cost. When Ali Salem gets married, he will be one of 650 grooms. 'If I got married by myself,' he said, 'I would need over £30,000. But if I go for this kind of wedding, I'll only spend around £10,000.' That is still a great deal of money.

7 Couples themselves can reduce costs by hiring wedding clothes. In particular, they should hire the bridal gown. In many countries, these dresses have hundreds of hand-sewn beads and crystals, and can cost thousands of pounds. However, a wedding dress is only worn once and then it is put away. It makes sense, therefore, to hire the dress for one or two days at a fraction of the cost.

A   Reviewing sentence structure

1. What can come after *and* in each sentence below from the text in Lesson 5.2? Think, then find an ending in the box below.

> crystals.   grooms.   it lasted three days.
> it made us very happy.   ~~relatives.~~   my house.
> their culture.   their families.   then it is put away.

   a. There is often a huge reception for all the friends and
      relatives.
   b. The expense is too high for many brides, grooms and …
   c. It was a traditional wedding and …
   d. It was beautiful and …
   e. I could spend the money on my child and …
   f. … if men marry out of their religion and …
   g. … ceremonies with hundreds of brides and …
   h. These dresses have hundreds of hand-sewn beads and …
   i. A wedding dress is only worn once and …

2. What is the information after *and*? Is it part of the object or complement? Or is it a new sentence?

B   Identifying a new skill (1)

1. Read the Skills Check.

2. The writer of the article probably has each opinion below. Find the section of the article which shows this bias.

   a. Weddings are too expensive in many countries.
      The writer says 'The expense is simply too high …'
   b. Men should only marry nationals.
   c. Governments should not make marriage with foreigners illegal.
   d. Governments should help couples to get married.
   e. People should not spend £10,000 on a wedding.
   f. The bridal gown should be hired.

C   Identifying a new skill (2)

1. Find three adjectives from the box which can go with each noun. (Some adjectives can go with more than one noun.)

> boring   busy   childish   crowded   hard   huge
> impossible   large   lengthy   lively   long   loud
> quiet   shy   tiny

   a. party   b. task   c. person   d. book   e. place

2. Which of the adjectives show bias?

   Example: *a **boring** party = bias = it is bad*
                  *a **lively** place = bias = it is good*
                  *a **long** task = no bias?*

Skills Check

Recognizing the writer's point of view

Why is this important? Because many writers are biased. They have an opinion which may not be based on facts.
A reader must recognize a writer's point of view, or **bias**, in an article.

Sometimes it is easy because the writer **states the opinion** or uses *must* or *should*:

Example:
*All governments **must** deal with the rising cost of marriage …*

Sometimes it is not so easy because the writer **implies the opinion**.

Example:
The text says,
*… there is often a **huge** reception …*

Perhaps the writer thinks,
*Receptions are often **too** large …*
because the adjective is very strong.

Recognizing the writer's bias helps to **evaluate the information** given.

Example:
The writer of the article in Lesson 5.2 thinks weddings are too expensive so only quotes people who are *unhappy* about the cost of weddings.

There are several patterns with *If*, including zero, first and second conditionals.
All the patterns describe actions and results.   ⑥

action			,	result			
S	**V**	**O/C**		**S**	**V**	**O/C**	
If / When	governments	ignore	problems		they	become	worse.	0
If	the government	changes / changed	the law	,	it	will / would	solve	the problem.	1 / 2

Which type of conditional describes:
• a hypothetical or unlikely action?   • a likely action?   • something that is always true?

Notes:
1. Sometimes writers do *not* put a comma at the end of the **action** clause.
2. All conditional sentences can begin with the **result** clause.

A   Recognizing conditional sentences in context
   1. Look back at the text in Lesson 5.2. Find and underline all the conditional sentences.
   2. What is the action in each case?
   3. What is the result? What modals are used instead of *will* in some cases?

B   Recognizing the form of conditional sentences
Find and correct the grammar mistake in each sentence.
   1. If you cool metal, it contracted.
   2. If you will heat water to 100°C, it boils.
   3. If an animal eats plants and other animals, it called an *omnivore*.
   4. If the climate changes too quickly in an area, some of the plants and animals may to die.
   5. If students get more than 70 per cent on average in all the assignments, they would get a first.
   6. People react badly if managers will treat them like children.
   7. You may remembered more if you highlight key words in your notes.
   8. I will move to a better flat if I had more money.
   9. Weddings would be a lot cheaper if people would not invite so many guests to the reception.
   10. The problem gets worse if the government will not take action.

C   Predicting the result clause in conditional sentences
   1. What do you expect to come next, in each case?
       a. If you heat metal, …
       b. If you drop ice into water, …
       c. If you don't do this assignment, …
       d. If you revise information regularly, …
       e. If you don't revise at all, …
       f. If I move closer to the university, …
       g. If I had more time, …
       h. If I owned a car, …
       i. If life expectancy continues to rise, …
       j. If a person has an autocratic management style, …
       k. If governments were more democratic, …
       l. If one part of a food web is removed, …
       m. If I was in charge of the country, …
   2. Which sentences above could also begin with *When*:
       a. with no change in meaning?
       b. with a change in meaning?

A **Activating ideas**

The average age of marriage in many countries, including the USA, has changed in the last 100 years. Why? Number these possible causes in order of importance, in your opinion.

☐ because of changes in technology

☐ because of an increase in wealth

☐ because of social conditions

☐ because of a change in the climate

☐ because of education

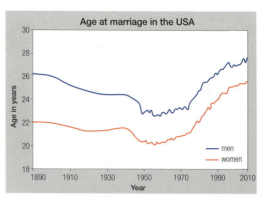

Age at marriage in the USA

American Academy of Political and Social Science

B **Preparing to read**

Read the assignment, then look at the article opposite – heading, photographs, topic sentences. Can you use the article in your research?

C **Understanding a text**

1. Read the article. Make notes for the tutorial.

2. What is the writer's opinion about the following? How do you know?

   • Rekha's actions

   • arranged marriages

   • the actions of Rekha's parents

   • the importance of education

Faculty of Social Science and Law

Tutorial: *Dowry and bride price*

There have been several articles recently in newspapers and magazines about arranged marriages, dowries and bride price.

Find an article which describes a recent case. Be prepared to talk about:

• location;

• events;

• wider social and legal issues.

Remember to check for bias in the article!

D **Understanding new words in context**

1. What do these phrases from the article mean?

   a. child labour
   b. prospective husband
   c. against the law
   d. underage children

2. Find the opposite of each word in the article.

   a. ordinary
   b. legal
   c. literacy
   d. acceptance
   e. causes
   f. allow

E **Developing critical thinking**

What is your opinion of the points in Exercise C2 above. Discuss in groups. Can you reach a consensus on each point?

The girl who said NO!

Rekha Kalindi is a 13-year-old girl who lives in a village in northeastern India. She is about 1.30m tall with long dark hair which she wears in a ponytail. She lives in an area with the highest female illiteracy in India. Her home has no electricity, no running water and no toilet. She goes to school like most 13-year-olds around the world. Rekha Kalindi is an ordinary poor Indian schoolgirl. However, in 2008, this ordinary young girl did something extraordinary.

When she was 12, Rekha Kalindi's parents arranged her marriage to a local man. But Rekha was not happy about the arrangement. She knew her future as a child bride. If she married the man, she would become a housewife and a mother, like her sister, Jyotsna. 'She got married at 12,' Rekha said. 'She is 15 now and she has already had four dead babies.' Rekha took a brave decision. She said no. The bravery of this young girl changed behaviour in her village and may change attitudes in her country in a dramatic way.

Rekha grew up in one of India's poorest villages and needed to work from an early age to help her family. She produced a kind of cigarette which is called a *beedi*. Then, in 2007, she was taken out of child labour and given the chance to learn in a government school. Many parents in India cannot afford to send their children to secondary school, but Rekha's school is free because it is supported by UNICEF. At school, she learnt the normal subjects of secondary students around the world. In addition, she had a course in leadership skills. It is possible that this course helped Rekha to make her difficult decision.

The arranged marriage between Rekha and her prospective husband was not a problem in itself. Arranged marriages are part of Indian culture, and many people feel that they work very well in most cases. Two families get together and agree that their children will get married at some time in the future. The arrangement was perfectly normal, but the marriage itself was against the law.

The Child Marriage Prohibition Act in India makes it illegal for girls below the age of 18 to marry. The same law forbids the marriage of males under the age of 21. However, a recent study in the UK medical journal *The Lancet* found that 44.5 per cent of Indian women in their early 20s were married by the age of 18. Of those, 22.6 per cent were married before they were 16, and 2.6 per cent before the age of 13. According to UNICEF, teenage pregnancy and motherhood is nine times higher among women with no education than among women with 12 or more years of education.

The law of India means that Rekha was right to refuse to go through with the marriage. But her refusal had huge consequences. Rekha's family were shocked by her action. They took her out of school, and even stopped giving her food for two weeks. However, Rekha did not weaken. People in the village began to talk about her, and then people in the state. Finally, she became a national news story. In the spring of 2009, the President of India asked to meet her. Clearly, the President saw her as a national symbol.

Rekha's decision was unusual but her original problem is not. There are very large numbers of marriages of underage children, particularly girls, all over the world. However, it shows the power of education. If more girls were educated, would more girls say no to illegal marriages? The answer is probably yes.

Level 3

PROGRESSIVE
Skills

Reading

Workbook

Workbook

A Predicting words from first letters

How can you continue each word, in the context of education? There may only be one way, or there may be two or more.

	noun	**verb**	**adjective**
1. under...	understanding	understand(s); understood	understandable
2. rem...	reminder	remember(s)/(ed); remind	
3. lear...			
4. forg...			
5. los...			
6. infor...			
7. intel...			
8. rese...			

B Word quiz

Find pairs of opposites in the box. Complete the table.

> ~~beginning~~ better change decrease difficult ~~end~~ fall forget go
> increase noisy put into quiet remain remember retrieve rise simple
> stay the same store take out of worse

beginning	end

C Word building: nouns and verbs; nouns and adjectives

Complete the tables.

noun	verb
a.	retrieve
b.	store
c.	design
d.	repeat
e. review	
f. memory	
g.	revise
h. process	
i. recognition	

noun	adjective
a.	bored
b.	thirsty
c.	hungry
d.	comfortable
e. noise	
f. tiredness	
g.	successful
h. introduction	
i. difference	

D Predicting words

Which words from Exercise C do you expect to complete each sentence? Make any necessary changes.

1. The human brain cannot remember everything. Forgetting is a natural _process_.

2. Research shows revision is the key to _____.

3. It is important that information is retrieved, used and _____.

4. We must repeat the cycle of retrieval – use – _____.

5. In other words, we need to have regular _____.

6. We must do this at regular intervals – ten minutes, one day, one week, etc. Mace called this 'spaced _____.'

7. But the general word for the process is _____.

E Collocations

Which noun(s) can follow each noun or adjective in the first column? Write one or more numbers next to each noun in the second column.

1. internal		brain
2. attention	1	factors
3. natural		grade
4. human		intervals
5. revision		opinion
6. test		period
7. learning		processes
8. scientific		research
9. regular		span
10. recent		style

F Grammar: finding the subject and object

Divide each sentence into subject (S), verb (V) and object (O).

        S   V   O

1. The arrival of gunpowder in Europe | led to | the end of castles.

2. The southern part of the country has many permanent rivers which provide drinking water.

3. The men and women from the winning team carry flags from the different areas of the city.

4. Recent studies at a number of universities show the importance of stable family life.

5. Children under the age of ten cannot usually understand mathematical problems which involve algebra.

6. The best-known research in the area of short-term memory was conducted by Miller in his 1956 study called 'The Magical Number Seven, Plus or Minus Two'.

G Reading line graphs

1. Look again at the text and graph on page 11 in the Course Book. Answer the questions. (Find the answers.)

a. What does the figure show?	Percentage of learning remembered.
b. Where did the information in the graph come from?	
c. What does the red line represent?	
d. How much information do you remember after six months with no review at all?	
e. What important thing happens during the first review?	
f. What are you going to do, as a result of reading this article?	

2. Look again at the text and the graph on page 15 in the Course Book. Decide if each statement is true or false. Correct any false statements.

a. The figure shows the percentage of learning in a lesson.	False. It shows the percentage of revision remembered.
b. The graph compares memory with regular breaks and with no breaks.	
c. The green line represents revision with breaks.	
d. You remember things better from the end of a revision period than the beginning.	
e. According to the article, you should stop for ten minutes at the end of an hour.	
f. You should take a break in the middle of a five-hour revision period.	

Workbook

A Wordsearch

Find 20 words from the unit in the wordsearch.

M	M	I	I	C	O	N	F	I	D	E	N	T	N	Y	U
I	N	S	T	I	T	U	T	E	Z	O	Z	E	E	N	Y
H	U	Z	C	P	R	J	H	I	S	H	Y	B	O	E	I
U	O	S	T	I	M	U	L	U	S	R	O	I	I	D	L
Q	R	R	A	R	I	S	E	L	T	W	T	D	N	D	V
G	E	M	I	E	I	T	V	A	L	U	E	O	F	Y	A
O	L	K	T	E	A	A	L	L	B	T	P	H	E	S	T
V	A	B	O	M	F	E	U	I	C	S	A	O	R	G	T
F	T	C	K	M	B	Y	R	E	E	C	R	P	I	V	I
B	I	R	H	E	K	T	P	R	T	N	E	E	O	P	T
K	O	L	R	D	N	X	E	C	S	J	N	L	R	U	U
W	N	J	E	O	E	U	E	U	R	N	T	E	M	B	D
H	S	K	C	N	X	L	W	X	C	M	B	S	G	L	E
W	H	Y	U	N	F	E	T	U	D	E	H	S	M	I	V
Y	I	K	F	E	G	A	F	A	C	C	E	P	T	S	F
Q	P	N	R	P	S	Y	C	H	I	A	T	R	Y	H	Q

1. rebel
2.
3.
4.
5.
6.
7.
8.
9.
10.
11.
12.
13.
14.
15.
16.
17.
18.
19.
20.

B Vocabulary

Use a word from the wordsearch in each of the sentences below. You may need to change the form.

1. Adolescents often _rebel_ against their parents.
2. Berne was director of an _____ in California.
3. He asked her a question and her _____ was unexpected.
4. How did the problem _____?
5. I am quite a _____ person. I always think I can do things well.
6. I don't like the way he behaves. His _____ is very bad, too.
7. People sometimes feel _____ to their colleagues.
8. There are often problems in the _____ between husband and wife.
9. Which company is going to _____ your book?
10. Young children usually _____ their parents.

C Life events

Complete each life event verb.

1. He was bo_rn_ in Australia in 1949.
2. He was ed_____ at a private school.
3. He st_____ Engineering at Melbourne University.
4. She g_____ from Melbourne in 1971.
5. He tr_____ as a civil engineer.
6. He pr_____ civil engineering in Australia for 30 years.
7. He de_____ several new ideas in engineering.
8. He fo_____ a school of engineering in 2005.
9. He di_____ in 2010.

D Predicting the next preposition

Each verb below can be followed by a preposition.

1. Which preposition? How do you expect the sentence to continue?

2. Find an ending for each sentence.

a. She looks …	to university next year.
b. He grew …	up in London.
c. I am going to apply …	after the library.
d. She trained …	of this exercise.
e. We moved …	with you.
f. I'd like to point …	as a psychiatrist.
g. She is acting …	to Australia in 1998.
h. The letters EU stand …	about his life at the moment.
i. I don't see the point …	as Personnel Manager in Alison's absence.
j. He is feeling good …	over as Training Officer?
k. Who is going to take …	for European Union.
l. It's really good working …	out a problem.

E Word power

1. What is the difference between each pair of words?

a. friend   acquaintance   _A friend is someone you know and like, whereas an acquaintance is simply someone you know._

b. psychiatry psychology

c. honest   reliable

d. accept   approve

e. grow   grow up

f. take up   take over

g. head   brain

h. say   state

i. print   publish

j. respect   like

2. Write one word or phrase from E1 in each sentence. You may need to change the form.

a. How can you make an _____ into a friend?

b. I know he's your brother but do you _____ of his behaviour?

c. Who _____ from Berne as director of the Transactional Analysis Society?

d. Some psychologists say that children _____ too quickly nowadays.

e. He _____ all his books with a small local company.

f. I _____ his ideas but I think he is wrong.

F Fixed phrases

What word often follows the word(s) below? Think of a word, then complete the expressions.

1. according ....
2. at the end ....
3. at that ....
4. in other ....
5. in this ....

6. as you can ....
7. do what you are ....
8. feel good ....
9. it won't happen ....
10. see the point ....

G Comprehension (1)

Look again at the text *Are you a Parent, an Adult or a Child?* on page 21 in the Course Book.
Answer the questions.

1. Where was Berne born?	
2. Why did he move to New York in the 1930s?	
3. Where did he develop his new idea about psychiatric problems?	
4. Why do people sometimes try to make other people feel bad, according to Berne?	
5. What are the three roles that people can take in Berne's model?	
6. What can a Parent do, in Berne's model?	
7. What about a Child?	
8. When do problems arise with transactions?	

H Comprehension (2)

Look again at the text *I'm OK, you're OK* on page 25.
Is each statement true or false? Explain the true statements. Correct the false statements.

1. Thomas Harris is American.	
2. He practised psychiatry in the Army.	
3. He taught Psychiatry at the University of Arkansas.	
4. Everybody feels good about themselves at the beginning of their lives, according to Harris.	
5. Everybody feels bad about other people at the beginning of their lives in Harris' model.	
6. The only healthy relationship for Harris is *I'm OK, you're OK*.	
7. If we think another person is not OK, we will not respect their contribution.	
8. We cannot change the way we feel about ourselves, or other people, according to Harris.	

Comprehension

1. Read the text *'Digest' problems to make good decisions* again on page 31 of the Course Book.
   Answer the questions.

a. What is the article about?	Making decisions.
b. How do you make a decision if you just rely on instinct?	
c. What does DIGEST stand for?	
d. Is DIGEST a mnemonic? Explain your answer.	
e. Why must you not evaluate at the same time as you generate ideas?	
f. How many alternatives does the writer give to the problem of arriving late for lectures?	
g. How could you evaluate the alternative possibilities, according to the text?	
h. What is the worst thing you can do in decision-making, according to the quoted saying?	
i. *Digest* in general English means 'break down food in the stomach so you can get the goodness out of it'. Explain the heading of this article.	

2. Read the text *Are you an autocrat or a democrat?* again on page 35 of the Course Book. Decide if
   each statement is true or false. Correct any false statements.

a. The article talks about two styles of management.	False – it talks about three: autocratic, participatory and democratic.
b. This article is only of interest to managers of companies.	
c. If you use the wrong management style, you may not achieve your objectives.	
d. The tables show you how to identify your management style.	
e. Your friends may not agree with your own idea of your management style.	
f. A person who makes fun of other people's solutions probably has a participatory management style.	
g. Most businesses were run by autocratic managers in the past.	
h. Most businesses are run by democratic managers nowadays.	
i. A democratic manager involves workers in selecting the best solution, whereas a participatory manager does not.	

E Word power: *do*

1. Which words and phrases can you use with *do*?
2. How do you expect each sentence with *do* to end?

   a. I'm really late. Could you do me a favour ?
   b. Edison, the American inventor, did thousands of
      ....
   c. Don't worry about the result. Just do ....
   d. I don't like that company at all. I don't want to do
      ....
   e. I bought the food so can you do .... ?
   f. She's a hard worker and she's doing a good
      ....
   g. How did you do in .... ?
   h. It was hard, but I did ....
   i. I asked him to help me but he did ....
   j. Do you use Wikipedia to do .... ?
   k. You look lovely. Who did .... ?

do	a job	
	your best	
	business with	
	someone a favour	✓
	a mess	
	the shopping	
	a mistake	
	your hair	
	good work	
	nothing	
	a deal	
	an exercise	
	an experiment	
	a promise	
	research	
	a test	
	well	
	a plan	
	the cooking	
	the right thing	

F Understanding non-text markers

Read the text opposite. Answer the questions.

Paragraph 1	1. What are *resources* in this article?	
	2. Which acronym is mentioned?	
	3. What do the letters of the acronym stand for?	
Paragraph 2	4. What are the important words?	
Paragraph 3	5. Which sentence is not completed?	
	6. How could you complete the sentence?	
Paragraph 4	7. What are the important words?	
	8. What is an expert?	
Paragraph 5	9. What is the quotation?	
	10. What does the quotation mean?	

G Understanding sentence structure

Look at the highlighted sentences in the text opposite. Complete the table.

	subject	verb	object / complement	extra words, phrases
Example:	we	must manage	our own resources	at those times
1.				
2.				
3.				
4.				
5.				
6.				
7.				
8.				
9.				
10.				

Teams work *with* teamwork

Sometimes we have to work on our own. At those times, we must manage our own resources – time, energy and money. We must also manage the task which is the job we want to do. However, we often have to work with other people, in a team. Teams can be very effective. But in a team, we need to manage ourselves, the task and the team. In other words, we must manage the TEAM (Time Energy And Money) in a team.

A team is not the same as a group. [1] A group is just a number of people. [2] For example, all the students in your class are a group. There are two main things which make a group into a team. [3] Firstly, a team of any sort has a particular *task*. It has an aim that it has to achieve. Everyone in the team should agree how to achieve the aim. [4] Secondly, each member in a team has a particular *role*. [5] In other words, each person must do a certain thing for the team. If the members do their roles effectively, the team will usually do its task effectively.

Let's take the example of a football team. The task of the team is to win. A football team wins when the players work together. The defenders stop the other side scoring goals. [6] The midfield players move the ball from the defenders to the attackers. The attackers score goals. If the goalkeeper tries to score a goal, the *other* team will probably score. If the attackers spend all their time defending, they probably won't score themselves. And if the players in the same team do not respect each other ...

[7] So the value of teamwork in *sports* is very clear. [8] But teamwork is also very useful in business and even in daily life. Researchers suggest that the best teams have at least three roles. [9] Firstly, all successful teams must have a **chairperson**. This person makes sure that the decisions of the team are followed through. [10] Secondly, a team needs **an expert** – a person with specialist knowledge in the area. This person helps the team to solve problems. Finally, **a team worker** is needed, to co-ordinate the work of the team members.

Teams work. They solve problems and deal effectively with issues. But team members must remember to respect team-member needs as well as individual and task needs. People sometimes say 'There is no *I* in team' but that is not true. Each individual member is important but the task and team are equally important.

H Fixed phrases

Choose a word from the box to complete each fixed phrase.

again	case	know	~~lot~~	place	say	this	time

1. a _lot_ of the time
2. again and ___
3. all the ___
4. as you ___

5. in a case like ___
6. in the first ___
7. in this ___
8. let's ___

I Understanding long sentences

Read the text. Find the second verb in each sentence. What is the subject (and verb / auxiliary / modal auxiliary) of the second verb? Is the second sentence negative?

Laissez-faire management style

There are three main kinds of management style and they are democratic, autocratic and participatory.	second verb – are; subject – they = the main kinds of management
However, there is a fourth style called *laissez faire*.	second verb – (is) called; subject = the fourth style
The name comes from two words in French and means 'leave to do' or 'leave alone'.	
Managers with this style give their staff complete freedom and do not interfere with their work.	
The best laissez-faire managers are available and help staff with problems, but do not give them solutions to their problems.	
Laissez-faire management can enable staff to develop and allow them to grow.	
In the best cases, staff become more motivated and learn to take responsibility for their own actions.	
However, laissez faire does not work in all businesses or motivate everyone.	
Some people cannot work with this kind of management or accept the lack of direct orders.	

A Predicting words

How can you continue each word, in the context of science and nature? There may only be one way, or there may be two or more. Write the word in the correct column.

	noun	verb	adjective
1. cli...	climate		climatic
2. des...			
3. pla...			
4. pol...			
5. hab...			
6. org...			
7. pyr...			
8. con...			
9. ada...			
10. eco...			
11. tro...			
12. env...			
13. end...			
14. ext...			

B What is the difference?

1. What is the difference between each pair of words in the table?

    A carnivore eats meat whereas a herbivore eats plants.

carnivore	herbivore
food chain	food web
consumer	producer
home	habitat
climate	weather
animals	living things

2. Write one word from the table in each sentence.

    a. An omnivore is both a *carnivore* and a _____.
        It eats both animals and plants. Humans, of course,
        are omnivores.

    b. All _____ breathe and respire. That is part of
        the definition.

    c. Animals can become extinct if there is a small change in their _____, for example,
        a small increase in average temperature.

    d. I really like the _____ here. Warm dry summers and cool wet winters.

    e. Most animals are part of a very complex _____ which involves many different animals
        and plants.

    f. There must be a _____ at the bottom of every food chain.

Verb + preposition

Write the correct preposition in each case.

1. Living things depend …		each other.
2. All living things are involved …		food webs.
3. Many animals are close …		becoming extinct.
4. In the first place, all energy comes …		the Sun.
5. Producer plants convert solar energy …		chemical energy.
6. Nutrition is obtained …		food.
7. Gaia is a theory put …		by James Lovelock.
8. All animals are adapted …		their environment.
9. Energy is transferred …		one living thing to another.
10. Decomposers break …		dead animals and plants into chemicals.

D Predicting with *which*

Match the beginning of each sentence with a relative clause.

1. Biomass is the name …		which a living thing occupies in an ecosystem.
2. A biome is a major environment …		which has less than 25 cms of rain a year.
3. A desert is an area …		which is given to stored solar energy.
4. Producers are plants …		which only eats plants.
5. Primary consumers are animals …		which covers a large area of the Earth.
6. A herbivore is an animal …		which convert solar energy into food.
7. A niche is a position …		which eat producer plants.
8. Photosynthesis is the process …		which is becoming extinct.
9. An endangered animal is one …		which no longer lives on Earth.
10. An extinct animal is one …		which converts solar energy into sugar, oxygen and carbon dioxide.

E General knowledge

Answer these questions from your own knowledge or memory of information from the theme.
Then check with the *Encyclopedia of Science* pages in the Course Book.

1. What is ecology?	
2. Why do living things depend on each other to survive?	
3. What can destroy an ecosystem?	
4. What is an environment?	
5. What happens if you remove one part of a food chain?	
6. Why is it difficult to predict the effect of a change in one part of a chain or web?	
7. Why are animals in a food chain sometimes put into a pyramid shape?	
8. How do fish in deep water adapt to their habitat?	
9. Is the Sahara Desert a biome?	
10. What is the Gaia hypothesis?	

A Predicting words from the first letters

What noun starts with each set of letters below, in the context of marriage?

1. we.dding..........
2. ma..........
3. ce..........
4. re..........
5. br..........

6. ho..........
7. hu..........
8. w..........
9. co..........
10. re..........

B Word power: verbs with *en*

Write a verb in each space with the meaning of the words in brackets.

1. Rekha's parents stopped giving her food but she didn't ..weaken.......... .	(become weak)
2. The road was too narrow so the council decided .... it.	(to make wider)
3. Steel .... by adding carbon.	(is made harder)
4. Your assignment is too long. You have to .... it.	(make shorter)
5. Athletes .... their bodies with exercise.	(make stronger)
6. In some countries, the school year is quite short and people are talking about .... it.	(making it longer)
7. How can the police .... that people do not break the law?	(make sure)
8. We must .... girls to complete secondary education.	(make possible for)

C Collocation

What can follow each verb? Match one set of possibilities to each verb.

1. reduce		a car / clothes / a person
2. arrange		a debt / a loan
3. deal with		a decision / an action
4. pay off		a marriage / a meeting / a loan
5. waste		a problem / a person
6. regret		a school / a decision / a person
7. hire		an offer / a loan / a request
8. change		behaviour / attitudes / customs
9. support	1	costs / temperature / weight
10. refuse		time / money / energy

D Money, money, money!

Write one word in each phrase connected with money.

1. to spend money .on..........
2. thousands of ....
3. extremely ....
4. a waste of ....
5. many people can't ....

6. all the wedding ....
7. take out personal ....
8. to pay off the ....
9. to share the ....
10. to offer ....

E What does it mean?

Writers sometimes use a general word for a group of things. They expect the readers to know the items in the group.

Example: The money goes on the bride's *wardrobe* and her *jewellery*.

dress, shoes, hat, etc.   rings, bracelets, brooches, etc.

What is the group of things in each *general word* below?

1. Student flats usually do not have much *furniture* in them. ....
2. We need to make sure that the *hardware* in the resource centre is up to date. ....
3. You must not use any *appliance* in your room until it has been checked by the Health and Safety officer. ....
4. Could you put out the *crockery* and *cutlery* on the dining table for me? ....
5. Safety *equipment* must be worn on this site. ....
6. The toy shop lost all its *stock* in the fire. ....
7. This computer is pre-loaded with basic *applications*. ....
8. A small number of *mammals* lay eggs. ....

F Predicting the second clause in conditional sentences

1. Cover the third column below. Read the start of each conditional sentence. What sort of information do you expect to come in the second clause?
2. Uncover the third column. Find a suitable clause to complete each conditional sentence.

a. If the government does not solve this problem		families would not need to take out personal loans.
b. If people are not educated		if the government offered incentives.
c. If couples get married very young		if they get married very young.
d. If the government increased the minimum age for marriage		if weddings were cheaper.
e. People might choose mass weddings	a	it will probably get worse.
f. If you hire the wedding clothes		some people would be very unhappy.
g. Girls may not finish their secondary education		they may make bad decisions about their own lives.
h. If bride price was lower in some countries		they may regret it later.
i. Couples would have more money to start their married life		you will reduce the cost a great deal.

G Paying the price of asking too much

1. Read the assignment. Read the text on the following page. Complete the notes for the tutorial below the text.
2. **CW** Compare your notes in pairs or groups.
3. The text has many long sentences which are joined with *and* or *but*. What is the missing subject of each highlighted verb?

Department of Media Studies

Topic 4: Bias in web articles

Choose a web article about a topical subject. Make a list of:
• the main **facts** in the article
• the **opinions quoted** in the article
• the **opinions** of the **writer** of the article – find evidence for your ideas

Be prepared to talk about the article at the next tutorial.

Paying the price of asking too much

Nisha Sharma is an ordinary woman but she is partly responsible for a rising trend in her home country.

In 2003, Nisha was 21 years old, a third-year student of Software Engineering at Indraprastha University in Delhi, the capital of India, and was hard at work on extra courses in her spare time. On May 11ᵗʰ, she was due to marry Munish Dalal, but just before the ceremony, her prospective husband was arrested and taken away along with his mother.

The union between Nisha and Munish was an arranged marriage. Arranged marriages are common in many cultures and are perfectly normal in India. Nisha was happy to marry Munish. 'I do not believe in love marriages' Nisha told us. Her family were prepared to pay a dowry. The Indian government tried to stop the damaging practice in 1961 when it made dowries illegal but it is still demanded by the parents of many grooms, and still paid by the parents of many brides.

The agreed price in this case was 15,000 rupees cash but was supplemented with other items, such as kitchen appliances, digital equipment and a brand new, gold-coloured car for Munish.

On the day of the wedding, Munish's greedy family went too far and asked for another 12,000 rupees in cash. 'When I said I didn't have that kind of money, they slapped me,' said Ms Sharma. The bride-to-be then took her brave decision and called the police.

Nisha's actions made the front page of newspapers across India, and led to congratulations from government ministers. 'If more girls acted like Nisha, this problem would start to disappear,' said a minister. In recent years, there have been other cases. For example, Anupama Singh walked out on her groom moments after the marriage when he asked for more money, and Farzana Zaki refused marriage the day before her wedding when the groom demanded more money and a house.

Today, Nisha Sharma campaigns for basic women's rights in India today. 'I hope,' she said, 'if women read about me, they will be inspired to act correctly. I call on every Indian girl to refuse to give a dowry. My experience has strengthened my belief.'

Opinions quoted
Nisha:
I do not believe ...

Main facts
May 11ᵗʰ 2003
Nisha   (21) to marry Munish

Writer's opinions
Arranged marriages:

Dowry:
Nisha's actions:
Women's rights:

A	a complete picture	1.1		efficient (*adj*)	1.1
	a great deal of	1.1		endangered (*adj*)	4.1
	acronym (*n*)	3.1		environment (*n*)	4.1
	affair (*n*) [= event]	5.1		Equator	4.1
	afford (*v*)	5.1		evaluate (*v*)	3.1
	approach (*n*) [= method]	3.1		evidence (*n*)	5.1
	arise (*v*)	2.1		expense/s (*n*)	5.1
	arranged marriage	5.1		extant (*adj*)	4.1
	at the same time	3.1		extinct (*adj*)	4.1
	attention span	1.1		extreme (*n*)	5.1
	autocrat (*n*)	3.1	**F**	feel good about	2.1
B	bias (*n*)	5.1		fixed (*adj*) [= attached]	1.1
	bored (*adj*)	1.1		food chain	4.1
	boredom (*n*)	1.1		food pyramid	4.1
	bridal (*v*)	5.1		food web	4.1
	bride price	5.1		forbid (*v*)	5.1
C	caption (*n*)	2.1		foreigner (*n*)	5.1
	carnivore (*n*)	4.1		forever (*adv*)	1.1
	chemical energy	4.1		found (*v*)	2.1
	child bride	5.1	**G**	generate (*v*)	3.1
	child labour	5.1		gift (*n*)	5.1
	clearly (*adv*)	5.1		gradually (*adv*)	1.1
	come up with (*v*)	3.1		grow up (*v*)	2.1
	concentrate on (*v*)	1.1	**H**	habitat (*n*)	4.1
	consequences (*n pl*)	5.1		heat energy	4.1
	consumer (*n*) [animal]	4.1		herbivore (*n*)	4.1
	contribution (*n*)	2.1		hire (*v*)	3.1, 5.1
	convert (*v*)	4.1		hunger (*n*)	1.1
	critically (*adv*)	5.1		husband (*n*)	2.1
	cross (*n*)	3.11	**I**	identify (*v*)	3.1
D	decide (*v*)	3.1		illegal (*adj*)	5.1
	decrease (*v*)	1.1		illiteracy (*n*)	5.1
	define (*v*)	3.1		imagine (*v*)	3.1
	democrat (*n*)	3.1		imply (*v*)	5.1
	desert [climate]	4.1		in reality	3.1
	destroy (*v*)	4.1		in the first place	4.1
	difficulties appear	2.1		incentive (*n*)	5.1
	discomfort (*adj*)	1.1		increase (*v*)	1.1
	do the right thing	3.1		inferior (*adj*)	2.1
	do what you are told	2.1		initial (*adj*)	1.1
	dowry (*n*)	5.1		instinct (*n*)	3.1
E	ecology (*n*)	4.1		internal/external factor	1.1
	economy (*n*) [= saving]	5.1		interval (*n*)	1.1
	ecosystem (*n*)	4.1	**J**	jewellery (*n*)	5.1
	edit (*v*)	5.1		journal (*n*)	5.1

L

loan (*n*)	5.1
logical (*adj*)	3.1
look after (*v*)	2.1
loss (*n*)	1.1

M

management (*n*)	3.1
management style	3.1

N

national (*n*) [= person]	5.1
natural process	1.1
note (*v*)	1.1

O

obey (*v*)	2.1
obvious (*adj*)	3.1
omnivore (*n*)	4.1
opinion (*n*)	5.1
organism (*n*)	4.1
overall (*adv*)	1.1

P

parent (*n*)	2.1
participatory (*adj*)	3.1
pay off	5.1
perfect (*adj*)	3.1
photosynthesis (*n*)	4.1
physical factor	1.1
polar [climate]	4.1
popular (*adj*)	5.1
possibility (*n*)	3.1
practise [= medicine]	2.1
process (*n*)	4.1
producer [plant]	4.1
prospective (*adj*)	5.1
psychiatric	2.1
psychiatry (*n*)	2.1
psychoanalysis (*n*)	2.1
psychoanalyst (*n*)	2.1
public transport	3.1

Q

quote (*n*)	5.1

R

rebel (*n* and *v*)	2.1
references (*n pl*)	5.1
reflect (*v*) [= show]	2.1
remain (*v*)	1.1
respond (*v*)	2.1
response (*n*)	2.1
retain (*v*)	3.1

S

saying (*n*)	3.1
see the point of (doing) something	2.1
sensible (*adj*)	5.1

share (*v*)	5.1
solar energy	4.1
source (*n*)	5.1
specialist (*n*)	5.1
state (*n*)	5.1
steeply (*adv*)	1.1
stick to (*v*) [= keep]	3.1
stimulus (*n*)	2.1
summarize	3.1
support (*n*)	5.1
survive (*v*)	4.1
switch (*v*)	2.1

T

take (*v*) [= get/catch]	3.1
take over (*v*)	2.1
temperate [climate]	4.1
the exact reason	1.1
the human brain	1.1
thirst (*n*)	1.1
tiredness (*n*)	1.1
tool (*n*)	5.1
transaction (*n*)	2.1
transfer (*v*)	4.1
tropical [climate]	4.1

U

(un)expected (*adj*)	2.1

V

validate (*v*)	5.1
value (*v*)	2.1
vary (*v*)	1.1
view (*n*)	5.1

W

waste (*n*)	5.1
weaken (*v*)	5.1
wife (*n*)	2.1
without thinking	3.1
work through (*v*)	3.1
worker (*n*)	3.1
workmate (*n*)	2.1